WRITING LEFT-HANDED

David Hare was born in Sussex in 1947. Upon leaving university he formed the Portable Theatre Company, which toured Britain for three years. He wrote his first play, *Slag*, in 1970, while Literary Manager at the Royal Court Theatre. Since then he has written twelve plays, of which seven have been presented at the National Theatre, and seven original screenplays for cinema and television. His first feature film, *Wetherby*, won the Golden Bear at Berlin in 1985.

by the same author

Plays
SLAG
THE GREAT EXHIBITION
BRASSNECK (WITH HOWARD BRENTON)
KNUCKLE
TEETH 'N' SMILES
FANSHEN
PLENTY
A MAP OF THE WORLD
PRAVDA (WITH HOWARD BRENTON)
THE BAY AT NICE
THE SECRET RAPTURE
RACING DEMON

Films for television
LICKING HITLER
DREAMS OF LEAVING
SAIGON: YEAR OF THE CAT
HEADING HOME

Films
WETHERBY
PLENTY
PARIS BY NIGHT
STRAPLESS

Opera
THE KNIFE

Writing
Left-Handed

DAVID HARE

faber and faber

LONDON · BOSTON

First published in 1991
by Faber and Faber Limited
3 Queen Square London WC1N 3AU

Phototypeset by Parker Typesetting Service Leicester
Printed in Great Britain by Clays Ltd St Ives Plc

Cover photograph printed by
kind permission of David Bailey

David Hare is hereby identified as the author of this work in accordance with
Section 77 of the Copyright, Design and Patents Act 1988.

A CIP record for this book
is available from the British Library.

ISBN 0 571 14334 2

Details of previous publications

Cycles of Hope: A memoir of Raymond Williams – *Guardian*
The Play is in the Air: On Political Theatre – Faber and Faber
Time of Unease: At the Royal Court Theatre – Amberlane Press
The Awkward Squad: About Joint Stock – *Granta* and Methuen
Now Think This Time: An Introduction to the History Plays – Faber and Faber
Why Pick on Us? An Introduction to the Asian Plays – Faber and Faber
Ah! Mischief: On Public Broadcasting – Faber and Faber
A Stint at Notre Dame: On Literary Fame – *Quarto*
Writers and the Cinema: On *Wetherby* – *Sunday Times*
Sailing Downwind: On *Pravda* – *Observer*
A Bit of Luck: On *Paris by Night* – Faber and Faber.

for Peggy

Contents

Introduction

It always amuses playwrights when writers from other disciplines discover for themselves how hard it is to write a play. Yesterday's playbills are marked with the names of some of this century's most distinguished poets and novelists who suddenly found the ground soft underfoot when condescending to the theatre. The form is, for some reason, uniquely deceptive. Most good theatre writing looks pretty easy. A good play seems to pass at such speed and with so little appearance of effort that novelists, exhausted by a more cumbersome form, fall to thinking that the whole thing must depend on some trick. I have even heard novelists threaten to 'dash a play off'. But the strange, necessary combination of vitality on the surface and power below – wave *and* tide, if you like – is harder than it looks. It is a mistake ever to write a play without giving your whole life to it. It can seldom be done left-handed.

This collection of essays is from my own left hand. I write prose very rarely. I have not written consistently for one publication, and a healthy proportion of what I submitted has been rejected by the people who asked for it. I explain elsewhere in this book that I discovered at the age of twenty-one that I had a facility for writing dialogue. But sentences which I intend purely for the page still look peculiar to me. I can't wait to hear them spoken out loud, preferably by somebody else, who is pretending to be somebody else again. Through my own carelessness, a number of unpublished pieces have been lost. I was asked to introduce the *Bedside Guardian* in 1986, but the result was thought too controversial for publication. Liberal newspapers in my experience invite you to be sceptical about everything except liberal newspapers. In the period after they unprotestingly betrayed her to the Treasury Solicitor, the *Guardian* found the words 'Sarah Tisdall' very hard to set up in type. A long article about the Falklands War was not accepted by the *Times Literary Supplement*, this time because it was not possible to say certain things about the Prime Minister. The *Financial Times* found no place for an article they had requested on politicians' use of language. Perhaps these editors were right. One unpublished piece is recovered here, however. It is an essay about Nick Bicât's opera *The Knife*. This was killed by *Esquire* who accidentally added insult to injury by enclosing an internal memo from a senior editor who said the piece 'did not really work'. Again, I am sure *Esquire* was correct. But, by a pleasant irony, I could not help noticing they planned to pay me more for writing an article about the opera than I had earned from directing the opera itself.

By chance, in the week after I had finished assembling this collection, I flew to Budapest where I attended an international writers' conference, sponsored by the Wheatland Foundation. Two days before we arrived, Imre Nagy, the most eminent victim of the Russian repression in 1956, was taken from his unmarked grave and re-buried with honour after a public ceremony in Heroes Square. Listening to the admirable speeches by writers from the Middle East and South Africa, it was clear that in countries ruined by war or dictatorship all the usual questions about art and politics easily resolve themselves. In Israel novelists and poets effectively *are* the opposition, at least to some of their government's more extreme policies. Yet the English writers were at the same conference the subject of a familiar attack from a literary critic, a fellow countryman who wished to argue that in Britain people had very little to complain about, and that looking proportionately at the horrors of the world, playwrights in particular would do better to celebrate the quality of life they enjoyed than to go on moaning about its few and occasional shortcomings. He argued that writers in England felt themselves powerless because they had sacrificed what he called their 'universality' in order to emphasize everything which is dark and depressing in modern life.

This is so common and confused a view that it is hard to know how to unpick what is truly a tangle of misapprehensions. The first mistake is to imagine that British writers, at least of my acquaintance, feel themselves in any way marginalized, or indeed that they wish to have any greater influence on the affairs of the nation than they have already. In my experience, they do not wish more than any other citizens to bring about the fall of governments, or to force laws onto the statute book. One of the great pleasures of writing for the theatre in this country is that the ideas you express can be taken so seriously and enter so smoothly into the currency of political discussion. If the theatre may be said to lack influence at all, it is more likely to be down to the quality of the work it produces than to any inherent prejudice against it in the population at large. The audience is there and waiting, if you have something sufficiently urgent to say and if – a massive if, in the life of this government – you are able to command the resources with which to say it. Indeed, if you want to understand the social history of Britain since the war, then your time will be better spent studying the plays of the period – from *The Entertainer* and *Separate Tables* through to the present day – than by looking at any comparable documentary source.

Furthermore there is something mean and patrician in the proposition that in countries which enjoy the right of dissent, it is the duty of writers to refrain from using it; as if freedom were not a right, but a privilege. Why should people fight so hard for this right if they are then to be told that it is immature to exercise it? In the company of so many writers who had been persecuted in their own countries, it became clear to me that writers, whether they intend to or not, serve much the same role in free as in totalitarian societies; they remind their audience of an alternative and perhaps more profound way of looking at experience than would otherwise be available. The degree of passion and skill with which they do this, and the effect they then have, may depend either on their circumstances or, goodness knows, on their character. But in each country the job ends up essentially the same. In writing about *The Knife* I introduce a huge subject into which I can make only the slightest inroad, but I try to suggest that morale-building orthodoxies are just as prevalent and just as insistently propagated in the West as in the East.

As to the charge that British writers in general stress unduly what is most disturbing in modern life, then I have to assume from the response of the audience to the variety of plays they see that a number of them share this interest, and identify with some of the dissatisfactions they see expressed. For myself, I was drawn into working in the theatre in what I wrongly took to be an apocalyptic time. In the opening lecture of the book, which is in part a memoir of my one-time tutor Raymond Williams, I describe a mood in the late sixties which had me decide that I wanted to set about dramatizing the crisis I then believed Britain to be in. In the second lecture, I describe some of the hard lessons I learnt in trying to make this impulse work in practice. Over the twenty years that I have continued writing, almost everything in my approach has changed. I have become fascinated by the formal problems of film and theatre, which once had no interest for me; I have moved from running small travelling groups to writing and directing on the largest stages I could find; and I have, in recent years, been drawn less to attacking the iniquities of a particular social system than to illustrating the dilemmas of all those who still struggle with the idea of what a good life might be.

In *Pravda* Howard Brenton and I tried to show that even if a man believes in nothing, he will always triumph over the man who cannot decide what he believes. Throughout the early 1980s liberal institutions were rolled over by their enemies, because they had no clue how to organize themselves to fight. The truly culpable figures in the wild comedy of the real-life Fleet Street take-overs were not the proprietors, who were after all only pursuing their own ends by their own standards, but the journalists and editors, who seemed not to know what on earth either their ends or their standards were. When I wrote *The Secret Rapture* I found I was drawing again, though more tentatively, on the same question, asking how destructive you need to become when dealing with destructive people. Neither of the sisters in the play is entirely good or bad. One, Marion, is a Tory MP who finds herself increasingly forced to pretend that life's problems are more simply soluble than they are. The other, Isobel, is trying to survive without a theory of evil among people who undoubtedly wish her ill. In *Strapless*, Lillian Hempel, an American doctor, is shown fighting to do a good day's work in the current National Health Service. And in *Racing Demon*, four clergymen try to make sense of their mission against impossible odds in the inner city. I feel I am only one among many when I say that, more and more, I find myself moved by people who have no apparent place in the much touted modern Western ethos, and who will never know any of its equally touted rewards.

Hemingway said politics in literature were the bits that readers would skip in fifty years' time. We all know what he meant. But a *sense* of politics seems to me no more nor less than part of being adult. When I first worked in the theatre, the prevailing fashion was for plays set in rooms, in which characters arrived with no past and no future. Human beings, it was implied, lived primarily inside their own heads. This seemed to me to offer not just a boring but an untrue view of life. In all the work I most admired, writers gave me a sense of how history pulls us this way and that, of how we live among one another, and how everything in our personal, even our spiritual lives is affected by how we came to be who we are.

*

Writing Left-Handed collects everything I have to say in my own voice. It is now easier to make a living talking about writing than writing. I make mild fun of this tendency in 'A Stint at Notre Dame', but the truth is I am more at ease working through invented characters. For better or worse, the theatre has been the dominant interest of my life, and for that reason I have excluded all my writing about what is called the real world. I wanted to focus on some of the common questions which are raised by a life of make-believe, and perhaps give an impression of how my views have changed with the passing of time. There is, in other words, an autobiographical thread. The essays are presented in roughly chronological order, not in the writing, but in the periods of my life which they cover. You find me first as a student at university and leave me, perplexed, trying to understand something about the actors who have given me so much pleasure.

One or two wild historical misjudgements have not been corrected. In particular, the passage in 'Writers and the Cinema' which predicts a brighter future for British films has, I hope, a gay period charm. I am also conscious throughout of the overuse of the personal pronoun. I have heard of a school where the boys counted the number of times visiting speakers said 'I', and awarded a narrow victory to A. L. Rowse over Field Marshal Montgomery – surely the most unexpected defeat of that distinguished soldier's life. But, as I have indicated, it is hard for a playwright not to think of prose as an extended dramatic monologue, sometimes, I'm afraid, for a semi-fictional character.

I would like to thank all those editors who have been kind enough to ask me to write for them. My views on the theatre, cinema and television have been sharpened in argument and greatly enriched by my friendship with my agent, Margaret Ramsay. First to last, she has been a touchstone for my work. For this reason, I am dedicating this collection to her.

CYCLES OF HOPE
A Memoir of
Raymond Williams

You wouldn't recognize Cambridge from when I went to study there in 1965. Awash with money and computers, rebuilt to accommodate wine bars and Laura Ashley, it stands now, its lawns trim, as tidy as toytown, wholly transformed from the seedy, neglected place I knew in what people of my age must now accept were the last of the post-war years.

I was an asthmatic, so for me Cambridge, with its chilling mists and slate-grey skies, was the worst possible place to finish my formal education. After leaving school I had filled in the six available months before university by flying Icelandic Air – stopover, Reykjavik – to California, where there still existed an exotic Pacific culture of mellow, sweet surfboards and girls who cut their jeans off round their thighs. The result was that I arrived at university in a thoroughly bad temper from which I never quite managed to recover. Convinced that I was doing the wrong thing, I forsook memories of the campus at Santa Barbara which gave straight on to the beach, to come instead, weak-chested, to study in a converted nunnery, built of flint, with Britain's leading Marxist, Raymond Williams.

In a later essay 'You're a Marxist, Aren't You?', Raymond makes great sport with how indiscriminately people now use that word. And of course he is right. It has become a genteel sort of insult. On certain lips 'Marxist' is used to cover for the much blunter 'communist', just as the squeamish say 'passing on' when they mean 'dying'. God knows, when at sixteen I had conceived the idea that I must now study with a Marxist, I had little idea of what such a person might be like. Temperamentally distrustful of establishments, I knew only that I must find someone who could teach me to make sense of my politics in my daily life.

I cannot say that my first sight of Raymond fulfilled my expectations. Here was an apparently genial man, who had for some reason adopted a manner older than his years. Looking at the biography in the front of one of his books, I realize now that he was only forty-three when I first met him, yet stories were already told of his once choosing to give a supervision with his naked feet in a mustard bath. His status and authority had prematurely aged him. His hair was swept back from his brow, his teeth were prominent, and he had a mild, lilting manner of speech. On the first day of our arrival he was telling us that we should probably not expect to see him again for another year. He was farming us out, as was his right, to his juniors, most of whom lived in terraced cottages on the outskirts of town. We would walk or bicycle to our new supervisors, in our tweed jackets, smoking our pipes, our wretched views on Wordsworth or the Metaphysicals tucked under our arms, all the time complaining bitterly of how we had been abandoned.

I had only chosen Jesus College because Raymond was there. I was scarcely drawn to it by its other distinctions which were two: a reputation for rowing, and for the existence of a prestigious club in which undergraduates and elderly dons pretended to be roosters together, clucking, making jokes about feathers and eggs, exhausting every available play they could on the word 'cock'. I could not have been more unsuited to the character of the college. Nor, I would have thought, could Raymond. Yet here he was, with his Marxist colleague Moses Finley, the distinguished ancient historian, two ferociously intelligent men, perched, conspicuous anomalies, non-oarsmen, non-hen-impersonators, using the college for nothing else but to teach. Or, in our case, not teach.

I was not entirely at ease with the study of English literature, and this was not wholly down to Raymond's reluctance to teach us. It was more particularly due to an aversion to the drawing up of lists. The study of literature at Cambridge was organized round the idea that our function was to give dignified approval to a collection of writers who were in some mysterious way held to be 'moral': George Eliot, D. H. Lawrence, Dickens, Jane Austen, William Blake. Approval was conversely to be withheld from another bunch who, if not exactly immoral, were nevertheless not positively 'moral' in the elusive Cambridge meaning of that word: Milton, Robert Graves, Evelyn Waugh, Thackeray, Trollope, Dryden, Sterne, W. H. Auden, Oscar Wilde ... oh yes, I hardly need say that the unapproved list turned out to be longer, and prosecuted with a vigour which was entirely missing in the defence of the approved. Wherein this 'moral' quality in literature lay, I was never able to discover, though it was bound up in something called 'seriousness' which seemed to be equally hard to define. The purpose of literature appeared to be to please critics. Writers should work to guidelines which must be in essence 'life-affirmative'. Yet in the Cambridge critics' own writing, there often seemed to be an academic meanness of spirit, which hardly affirmed life at all.

Somewhere in the middle of my second year, I reached a turning point in my education. I was being instructed in aesthetics by a don from another college, who came out and said bluntly what I had long suspected. He informed me, as

3

an absolute law, that profound feeling could only be stirred in people by first-rate works of art. Only by coming to understand what was the very best, and then coming to value it above all things, could readers experience the deepest satisfactions of art. I asked him where this left people who enjoyed a profound religious experience when contemplating the work of an artist whom superior people held to be bad. I gave Salvador Dali as an example. The don's scorn was complete. 'Anyone who when looking at a painting by Salvador Dali imagines himself to be experiencing anything is quite simply wrong.' *Wrong?* 'They are fooling themselves. They may think they are having an experience, but they are not.' *They are not?* 'Only worthwhile works of art can produce worthwhile emotions.' But, I said, pressing a little further, who is the legislator for the worthwhile? Who is to define 'worthwhile'? He looked at me as if the question answered itself. 'Well, me. And people like me,' he said.

It would be fair to say from this point on I lost a good deal of relish for my studies. I had no desire to train to be a non-commissioned officer in the arts police, patrolling literature for capital offences such as 'failure of seriousness', or 'writing while under the influence of immorality'. The attitude of my don implied such a contempt for the ordinary feelings of people that the inevitable result of all this list-making would surely be more to remove me from life than to plunge me into it. Outside the university, a Labour government was once more selling its own supporters down the river, the Americans were snared in an insane war in Vietnam, middle-class youth throughout the world was bursting with indignation. What on earth could this *judging* be to do with anything?

I suppose this is how I came to think of the theatre as real. The critical and the creative came to seem to me diametrically opposed. If the purpose of criticism was indeed to inform people that they had no right to enjoy what they had hitherto been enjoying, then the purpose of writing a play or a novel was surely to greet them with something they might recognize and find they liked, almost in spite of themselves.

In this matter Raymond was an unusual professor, for in his own critical volume on tragedy he included in the back of the book a play about Stalin, which he had written himself. It was widely held to be unperformable – as far as I know, it's not been seen on a stage – and yet there was in the act of his including it a foolhardiness which at once made him personally attractive. It was hard to imagine any other don who was willing to forsake the safety of telling dead writers what was wrong with their work to risk making a fool of himself by writing his own play.

We would see Raymond across the quadrangle, books under his arm, a Dylan cap worn at an unlikely angle on his head, entirely in a world of his own, waving and running if one of us caught his eye, and we began to understand exactly why he had not wanted to waste another year dragging yet another generation of students through the novels of Thomas Hardy. It was clear from his book. He wanted to write.

Only in the third year did his students finally confront him. He had become so agile at avoiding us that when we turned up at the beginning of term there were no plans even for the usual cursory meeting. Instead, we were instructed to report to an old colleague of his, this time actually outside the city limits. Our suggested tutor was chiefly known for his highly coloured campaigns against eroticism in literature. He spent much of his time counting four-letter words in novels, and consulting with Swedish psychotherapists who had theories about the long-term mental damage done to people who had become addicted to reading descriptions of the physical act.

He had published a letter in the *Guardian* about the links between Hitlerism and nudity. He was widely held to be utterly cracked. It was typical of Raymond's mood at the time that he was more concerned to help out an old friend who was in need of a few quid from tutorials than he was to prepare us for the rigours of the tripos exam.

I have since been reminded that what followed was a strike. I'm not sure. Were things really that dramatic? I remember only an ultimatum. His third-year students told Raymond that they had been lured to the world's dampest university on false pretences. They had come for his personal tuition, and they were going to sit in his rooms until he consented to give it. I do remember his discomfort, which was profound. In the autumn of 1967, it was not an easy situation for the intellectual leader of the academic left to find himself in. It was downright embarrassing. In London new radical newspapers were being started. New political factions were forming in an atmosphere of wild optimism and vitality. The organized and disorganized left were taking to the streets. There was barely a new grouping that did not want Raymond's blessing and guidance. Yet on his own home ground his concentration was being disturbed by a small, self-righteous bunch of students who were demanding instruction in a subject in which they did not even any longer believe.

It was, I think, our scepticism about the study of literature which particularly infuriated him. To him it was self-evident that the professional study of literature was worthwhile and rewarding. He had no doubts, for his personal experience allowed him none. He had been a working-class boy from the borders of Wales. Literature and its study had been for him the way out of his environment but, much more important, it had also been the means by which he had understood his own feelings about that environment. Acutely sensitive to personal

6

suffering, Raymond remained throughout his life fascinated by social history. I have no proof of this, but I believe that he was drawn to his favourite subjects – the industrial revolution, the movement of people between town and country – because of his passionate concern that people who might otherwise finds themselves victims of history should be able instead to understand their own circumstances. And there was, self-evidently to him, no fuller way to understand than through imaginative literature. It had done the trick for him. As a young man, it had broadened and expanded him. In a Welsh grammar school, it had helped him to find meaning in his own upbringing. But now a generation of middle-class students was appearing at Cambridge whose attitude to literature, to the stuff itself, was a good deal more ambiguous.

It is easy now looking back to see myself only as a pre-cocious and shallow young man who confused the study of literature with literature itself. I became so contemptuous of the list-makers that I came to believe that the books they listed could be of little practical use or value in trying to understand the present day. Because the critics' lists seemed so irrelevant to anything I understood as urgent or worth-while, so I became suspicious of the claims of art, and merely amused by the personalities of those who made a living from it. A similar distemper marked my politics. Britain was trans-parently in crisis. Its institutions were bankrupt. Its ruling class was anathema. Its traditions were a joke. A favourite game among undergraduates of my year was to spend long, restful evenings arguing about where a single campaign of aerial bombardment might be directed to best effect: on Buckingham Palace, on the Palace of Westminster, or in the mean square mile of the City of London. There was rarely in our discussions any time for all the finer points of socialist theory which made up Raymond's work and life. Only one bright, shining idea was misappropriated from Marxism and given universal assent: that from its own terminal contradictions, Western society would surely burst asunder in an orgy of violence and civil unrest. What would then happen nobody could say.

Nothing in Raymond's behaviour so attracted my scorn as his decision in the winter of 1967 to bury himself away in his room and set to work with a team of curly-headed academics who arrived from London in Citroëns to edit a project entitled *The May Day Manifesto*. This work, to be published on 1 May 1968, was to set out a comprehensive programme of socialist change for the Britain of the 1970s. A yellowing copy of the eventual Penguin Special still sits on my shelves, a reminder of the days when, as a sort of Sergeant Pepper album of the organized left, it offered me and my despairing chums a fathomless source of satirical energy. As students, we took from Raymond the well-made point that an 'idea', so called, is not anything manufactured by an intelligentsia behind closed doors, but is more truly the expression of a widespread feeling which has arisen among many people at a particular time, and which then needs to be articulated. But if, as Raymond so often insisted, culture was in that way ordinary, then why did a manifesto of political ideas have to be set out in precisely that excruciating jargon which has alienated so many potential supporters from an interest in socialism?

The matter of Raymond's style remained a mystery to me for many years. Why, for heaven's sake, could he not be clear? Or rather, why did he choose to write in a manner which could only be understood by other highly educated people, or by those already versed in the modish junk terminology of left-wing politics? Here was a man who believed that ideas should belong to the whole population, whose own best work had sprung out of his time as an adult education tutor, yet who persisted in ploughing through the English language as through a field of dry bones, periodically using his favourite words 'long' and 'complex' to justify the tortuousness and complication of his sentences. How could this highly sophisticated man not see that unless he laid his thoughts out clearly and simply in everyday language, he had no chance of reaching the very people whose interests he sought to advance?

But it was not simply to the style of this enterprise that his students objected. It was, as we believed, to its fatal lack of realism. We could not see the point of spending the winter months in putting together a detailed programme for change in Britain when it had not the slightest chance of being effected. Anyone who was brought up in the fifties had a very clear understanding that they were a member of one of the most deeply reactionary societies in Western Europe. The high-flown ideas of a group of Cambridge intellectuals had not the slightest chance of influencing the statute book, nor of forming the revolutionary programme of some putative army which, before advancing down Oxford Street to seize the Post Office Tower, would pause in its stride to consult a small red book about what it should be doing in its first weeks in control.

Politics, in our view, was about power. And power was about property. England, pre-eminently in the British Isles, then as now, was a vastly rich country, in which the ownership of land and buildings was grotesquely disproportionate. It was childish to imagine that the huge vested interests of property and money would surrender a penny of their wealth without the bloodiest of armed struggles: and it was also childish and immature not to foresee that the outcome of any such struggle would be chaotic and unruly. Even if – a massive if – you momentarily allowed the possibility of revolution in this most unlikely of settings, then you would, in looking at other revolutions, see only a record of theory being thrown away and burnt in a high-octane mix of happenstance and *real-politik*.

Nothing prepares us for this, and nothing makes us sadder, than the moment when we realize that, in England, the fight is to the death.

If I suggest that I was able to articulate this in my relationship with Raymond, let alone sit and argue it with him, then I do wrong to his memory. For we were simply two different animals, who sniffed distrustfully round each other: he always drawn to the long view of things, patient, discriminating, qualifying every sentence with another sentence, pointing up historical parallels in every situation, set and determined in the sifting process which was his life's work; me, wanting to be tough and weeping for change.

The experience of the twenty years which have since gone by has done little to change my instinctive view of things, though I would hope it has deepened it. I am less impulsive. If you ask me for the reasons for the chronic problems of reaction in the British, then it is to the character of their intimate lives, their attitude to their children, their ways of giving and failing to give love, to their uncertainties and crises of spirit I would look, rather than rely on the much more materialistic outlook I had when I was young. But those same twenty years have also vindicated an impression I had then, that we were about to embark on a period of history in which British public life would be marked out by one thing: that, as a people, we cannot agree on anything.

I am trying to suggest that my character and Raymond's, ostensibly so different, were in fact shaped by our varying emotional responses to a common set of facts. For one thing also distinguishes those who seek change in Britain: an overwhelming sense of their own powerlessness.

Recently in Rome, looking at the Church of St Peter, I found next to the altar two statues, the masterpieces of Gugliemo della Porta, representing the figures of Justice and Prudence. In the original carving Justice had been nude. But her figure was so astonishingly beautiful that in the nineteenth century priests used to gather and become aroused by her. So, predictably, the Pope had ordered her to be clothed. And now, one hundred years later, her true figure is still hidden from view, for fear that if Justice is seen naked, she will drive the people crazy. This perfect parable, as eloquent perhaps about the Roman Catholic Church as it is about the beauty of Justice, underlies the life of all those who share a belief that things are not ordered in our country as they might be: that privilege is still unequally distributed and above all, that British institutions show no wish to be sensitive to more than one section of the population.

Raymond's response to this powerlessness was to set himself upon a life's work of patient elucidation. In his commitment, he was quite extraordinarily stubborn. When in 1964, Harold Wilson was elected Prime Minister, Raymond had infuriated his excited students – I have this only at second hand – by warning them that, like all previous Labour administrations, this one would now proceed systematically to betray both the people who had voted for it and the principles to which it had claimed to adhere. The students had better prepare now, on the night of victory, for the coming years of disillusionment, and steady themselves for a longer and longer fight. As in subsequent years he was proved so spectacularly right, then the attitude of his students hardened not into one of gratitude for his prescience, but into heartfelt resentment of this wise old bird whose passion for the moment seemed always to be elaborately qualified by his exquisite sense of history. Where was the fun? And where was the anger? If, as he believed, democratically elected governments were always pulled to the centre by the power of capital and the suffocating influence of traditional institutions, then where could young men and women get their hope for the future? Not, surely, in a life spent behind high walls, in the chilly Fens, grading Herbert against Donne, and discussing defects of style in comparative English literature.

For, yes, after our protests, after our sit-in, after what others have called our strike, Raymond reluctantly agreed to teach us. It is the governing irony of this memoir that I can now barely recall a single thing he said to me during the supervisions we finally spent together. It brings back something of the flavour of the times to remember that we insisted on his personal tuition not because we genuinely wanted to listen, but, more typically, because it was our 'right'.

I cannot excuse myself for the time I wasted being angry with Raymond. I was too stupid to realize that he understood me better than I understood myself. Attending an undergraduate production of *Uncle Vanya*, I identified with Vanya's anger at his one-time professor, the insufferable Serebyakov, in whom the young Vanya has believed and by whom he feels himself betrayed. For years nothing disturbed the self-righteousness of my version. Yet the truth of the situation was more nearly that I was too exercised and confused to take whatever help Raymond might have offered me.

Only one remark of his do I remember. After a particularly incoherent dissertation from me on the works of D. H. Lawrence, there was a long and moody silence. Raymond sat for a while, staring at my week's work, then took his pipe from his mouth, shook his head, and said, 'Lawrence, poor bugger. Poor bloody bugger . . .' He then put my essay down without any further comment at all. This judgement from the most gifted social and literary critic of his time on the foremost novelist of a previous generation has always seemed to me to carry a singular, even a definitive authority.

Soon after tripos, I was off. While my friends were on the barricades in Paris, I was sitting in a hot exam room, not quite fulfilling the rich promise which the college had detected in me when it had given me a scholarship three years before. With Tony Bicât, who had passed a similar three years in the same college, spending a sizeable personal inheritance on good suits and becoming a jazz drummer, I arrived in London to work first at Jim Haynes' inspirational Arts Laboratory, where young men and women could put on the plays they liked, in the way they liked, in order to shock an audience who had seen it all. One night, trying not to disturb a couple who were making love on the floor of the single dressing room in which our actors were preparing to go on, Tony and I resolved to make some sense of our convictions by taking theatre out of the metropolis and to all sorts of places where it was not usually expected. Another night, soon after, the only person in the auditorium was a large, genial man who seemed unsurprised to find himself the only member of the audience. Taking advantage of the tradition that a company need not perform when it outnumbers the spectators – in this case by a ratio of five to one – we suggested that we go, audience and actors, to the local pub, where for the first time I was introduced to Howard Brenton.

Often in my life I have thought I was breaking violently with the past only to discover a continuity which was apparent to everyone but me. In setting up a new travelling group, Portable Theatre, I believed I was putting Cambridge behind me as decisively as I could. How then do I explain that the first plays we chose to present to bewildered audiences in

church halls, army camps and on canteen floors up and
down the country were taken from the diaries of August
Strindberg and Franz Kafka? Yes, there was a foreign tilt of
which Cambridge moralists would not have approved, morality being the peculiar property of the British, but, even so,
what reaction were we expecting with such neurotic and
abstruse material?

Only with Howard's arrival did we begin to look towards
our own times. Even he had trouble getting there. He had
originally planned to write a history of evil from Judas
Iscariot to the present day – I drafted the publicity sheet, so
the phrase rolls effortlessly off my tongue – and yet he found
himself obscurely obsessed with the figure of the mass
murderer, John Reginald Christie, whom he resolved, for
the purpose of the drama, to bury every night under a
mound of screwed-up newspaper in a pen of chicken wire.
With this startling image – Christie, in a darkened theatre,
rising from his grave, holding the length of piping he used to
gas his victims – Portable Theatre found itself and was truly
born.

I now see the company as an early attempt to side-step the
problems of aesthetics. To an extent the theatre will always
be a magnet for hobbyists, people who are drawn like
train-spotters or matchbox fans to compare different performances of *Hamlet*. They form, if you like, a core audience, who survive over the years. Their overriding interest is
in the maintenance and improvement of their collections,
and so they will direct their attention not so much at what is
said, as at the skills which are being used to say it. As young
men, neither Tony not I had any wish to have our work seen
as being part of the English theatre. We wanted the
audience to concentrate not on whether we did or did not
belong with other groups and movements, nor on how our

production standards compared with others', but instead on the violent urgency of what we had to say.

Raymond himself approaches this problem in what I still take to be his greatest essay 'Culture is Ordinary'. He attacks the use of the word 'good' in a morally neutral context. He points out that people say a 'good' job has been done when they mean it has been professionally carried out, regardless of what the job was, and what ultimate effect it would have. In this sense Nazis might produce a 'good' newspaper. Or military leaders might sophisticate 'good' methods of torture. In Raymond's view a thing cannot be good unless it has a morally good aim. To those of us who worked for Portable Theatre in the late sixties, a 'good' play could only be one which shocked and disturbed an audience into realizing that the ice they were skating on was perilously thin. Any other kind of play could only be a distraction. Perhaps you may feel now that we were a little narrow-minded. Yet even today, when my mood is less apocalyptic, try as I may, I find myself indifferent to the bulk of English theatre, in which the same old plays are aimlessly revived, and the shelves of the London Library are combed for the obscurest examples of seventeenth-century writing. Shakespeare and his contemporaries did not sit around discussing whether it was worth reviving *Gamma Gurton's Needle*, and whether it worked in modern dress. They were arguing about which of them should write the next play.

Our way of focusing the audience's attention on our message rather than our means was to deny ourselves the luxury of finesse by tumbling a group of actors out of a van into an apparently unsuitable space with only the crudest and most makeshift scenery. Most of the plays were short, subversive and aggressive. Once, in Workington, the audience were still seated, waiting for us to take a curtain call, even as our van sped beyond the city limits and away down the motorway.

In the years to come, newspaper journalists would cotton on and start to write much windier analyses of the politics of decline. Antagonists went straight from calling us hysterical to calling us passé. By the time we had presented a series of these plays, all round the country, arts centres were beginning to spring up. The new audience we had deliberately sought were beginning to find themselves plugged in to what came to be called a circuit. The bureaucratic nightmare of a centrally controlled Arts Council funding, with the attendant apparatus of boards, sponsorships and five-year plans, began to lock the performing arts in Britain into an intractable grid. And suddenly, when we were told that our costumes were better than the Freehold's but that our lighting wasn't as good as Pip Simmons', we realized that aesthetics, like the sea, covers everything, and will always have its revenge.

I lost touch with Raymond, and I cannot say I thought much about him. When I was writing with Trevor Griffiths, who frequently referred to him, I remember being astonished that anyone who worked in the theatre should think it worthwhile to maintain a dialogue with dons, even with one who was himself a creative writer. Theatre was doing. Academics were children, who worked in an unreal world of their own making. They were spared the minute agony of seeing their ideas fail in front of an audience. Unlike playwrights, for whom every night brings unwelcome scrutiny, they could live inside their own illusions, talking only to one another in their private language. I thought of them as not grown up. Besides, Cambridge was flirting with something called structuralism, which downplayed the individual's imagination, and insisted that the writer was only a pen. The hand, meanwhile, was controlled largely by the social and economic conditions of the time. This depressing philosophy was not one to cheer the heart of a playwright. It was indicative of the way academics were once more turning their faces to the wall. The other day, one of the wittiest and cleverest structuralists in England, an ex-pupil of Raymond's, told me the whole thing was over. 'Oh great,' I said. 'Does that mean I'm back in charge of my own work?' He looked at me a moment. 'Mostly. But not entirely,' he said.

Meanwhile, civil violence not having broken out in the way I had predicted, I found myself making crab-like progress towards two of the central institutions of the culture, fascinated by the challenge of how to write plays which filled up the huge stages at the National Theatre, and delighted at the opportunity of reaching the huge public who still watch drama on the BBC. When I argued with another television playwright that the audience was not sitting there in one lumpen mass, passively receiving everything and unable to distinguish between the programmes and the advertisements, I was, in my insistence that the audience can and do discriminate, unknowingly parroting Raymond. It was so long since I had read him that I imagined my ideas were my own.

In 1983, fifteen years had gone by since I had last spoken to my former teacher. Out of the blue, I was invited to the Cotswolds, where Raymond was to give the keynote lecture at a forthcoming literary festival. I was asked if I would attend, and then without preparation join him on the platform to give my view of what he had just said. By the happiest of chances, we did not even meet before his talk, so I had no idea of what was to come.

He started hesitantly, drawing on a passage from *The Long Revolution* to detail the W. H. Smith bestseller list of 1848. Of the books listed not a single one was remembered, except for one by Jane Austen, who managed to come in at number eight. Taking the moral from this, Raymond drew attention to the extraordinary fertility of artistic activity in the world today, and to the breakdown of the old categories. Demographically the world had expanded beyond recognition, so there were more artists practising than at any time in history. Wonderful poems were being written in the West Indies; great novels were coming out of Nigeria; from India came great films; in Britain the theatre was lively as never before. In the face of all this activity, he said, the critic had great difficulty concealing his anger. So much going on! And all out of control! The critic's first instinct was to resent so much energy, for energy is the enemy of order, and order is the critic's job. No sooner had he or she written his piece on the death of the novel than the novel turned out to be bursting with life in Latin America. Moving quickly to come to terms with that, the critic now found himself wrong-footed by being told of something even more interesting going on in Czechoslovakia. Modern writing was unruly in its sheer abundance. Nobody could put a value on anything.

How then was a critic to react to this apparent chaos? Raymond smiled. By embracing it, he said. Let's not worry too much, let's just be grateful. Let's not succumb to the myth that there's no great writing any more. Every generation of critics asks you to believe that. They will always pretend that they knew which one was Jane Austen all along. But here it is, a matter of historical record, that Jane Austen once went unremarked, one among many, no more and no less popular than many of her fellow novelists. Let's not endlessly complain about what's not being done. Indeed, if we feel so strongly, then let's do it ourselves. Let's not peddle all that tired stuff about standards. Let time make judgements, as surely it will. Meanwhile, for goodness' sake, let's celebrate what we have.

I have never seen Raymond's lecture written down, so if my

paraphrase is selective, you must forgive me. You may detect, for instance, that the tones of our two voices have become merged. But this only reflects an excitement I felt when I realized that after so much misunderstanding, he and I were, in the vaulted hall of the Cheltenham Literary Festival, for the first time in our lives, about to see eye-to-eye. But I do not misremember the conversation that followed over cups of tea, in green china. 'Yes,' he said, 'you were right. And I knew you were right, when you argued that the study of literature as it was then practised at Cambridge was a worthless activity. Underneath all that judicious grading of literature lay an actual hostility to literature itself. But . . .', he said, '. . . at that time I could not admit it. For to admit it was to allow my own irrelevance. Only since I've given up teaching have I been able to see those years for what they were.'

Laughing together, we both relished the symmetry. While he had been travelling in my direction, I had been travelling in his. 'My politics at that time were a joke,' I said. 'I was so incensed, so personally outraged with the discovery that the country's leaders had no clothes on, that I could not imagine that my outrage was not universally shared. I could not understand why you, as a socialist, seemed so sanguine, so ready to go on discoursing in your own little world. Aflame with indignation, I projected that indignation onto my fellow countrymen and assumed violence was inevitable. But I've learnt since, in the long years of Heath and Callaghan and Thatcher, that a country may despise its leader with one part of its brain, and obey him or her with the other. Although I still love the power of that impulse which saw us all out on the streets shouting our heads off, I have also begun to value at last the quieter and more profound discernment which your kind of work represents.'

In any work of fiction which climaxed with this touching

scene, pupil and teacher reunited after fifteen years and each envying the other the choices they had made, the two characters would be used to represent different qualities. Most conveniently it would be said that Raymond represented careful reason, and that I represented ignorant feeling. Yet to paint it that way would be to do Raymond the gravest injustice.

An academic who can begin an essay on culture with his own childhood bus journeys from Hereford Cathedral into the Black Mountains is already set apart from most of his colleagues in his understanding of what is important. Underpinning everything Raymond wrote is a sense of possibility. Men and women cannot begin to fulfil the potential of their imaginations, unless they are allowed to influence and control their working lives. A society cannot be healthy unless the thoughts and feelings of working people are given the same cultural status as those of a privileged middle class. The impulse which moves Raymond's work all the time is one of deep emotional generosity, a readiness to share in the pleasures he had enjoyed, and a delight in watching other people come to value them.

In his writing he mixed this with a passion for the absolute truth. Only when you grasp this can you understand the problems of his style, even if you cannot forgive them. Reading his books is often like finding the world's most exciting ideas somehow trapped under the ice. It was Tony Bicât who finally revealed to me that he too had been mystified by the manner of Raymond's writing, until he realized that its very cumbersomeness came from a horror of conventional thinking, and an absolute determination to make a sentence mean exactly what it meant and nothing else. Raymond could be simple when he wanted to. But he rarely did.

It is the fashion now to denigrate the sixties. Trendy right-wing politicians, in hollow affectation, pretend to trace this country's ills to those days. They talk about the loosening of social bonds, and the decline of respect. In a favourite joke of Raymond's, a class which throws its own male children out of its homes, aged seven or thirteen, is in a poor position to lecture others on family values. As the period of office of the Thatcher government gets longer and longer, so the excuses for its failure must be traced further and further back in time. We are told that the deep-rooted problems of British life stem from the sixties. The word 'deep-rooted' is used to mean 'before we came to power'. Humourless themselves, the politicians cannot understand that a sense of the ridiculous is precisely what motivated most of what went on at that time. A lot of us do not need to be told, twenty years later, that our behaviour was ridiculous. Most of us knew it perfectly well at the time. That was part of the point. The reason no actor has ever given a successful or unembarrassing performance of a hippie is the same reason no one will ever play Groucho Marx or Jimmy Durante successfully: you cannot impersonate people whose whole gift is for satirizing themselves. The clothes, the hair, the language are now spoken of as if the inventors of these customs did not know that a joke was in the air. Yet the absurdity, both in Europe and America, did have a certain purpose. Everyone was angry. But for a while, they used their sense of humour to turn away despair.

I did not see Raymond again, yet when I read of his death I could not believe another five years had gone by. Our meeting seemed fresh, for the comfort it had given me lasted in a way that took no account of time. A struggle had been resolved. And now he had died.

In writing this memoir, I have suggested that this relationship between us had some special significance. I now have no way of knowing what it meant to Raymond, nor would I ever like to have asked. I was only one of the thousands of pupils who passed through Raymond's hands and, for reasons I have tried to make clear, not one with whom he was especially engaged. His last words to me were to complain of the ubiquity and neediness of his acolytes. 'I can't be a father to everyone,' he said.

Last December the college which had once threatened me with expulsion invited me to be guest of honour at the Annual Fellows Dinner. In the Upper Hall, surrounded by the portraits of famous scholars and benefactors, I reminisced with a senior tutor, who told me our experience of Raymond refusing to teach us had been repeated many times in Raymond's later years. I asked if the college had done anything about it. No, he said, we accepted that a college like this should be magnanimous enough to give him its protection without insisting he fulfil his official obligations. 'Besides,' he said, 'we didn't have his telephone number.'

*

It is good to come here today and talk as truthfully as I can about what passed between us, happily in front of his family and friends, and in the part of the world where he was brought up. Yet the occasion is, as ever, kissed with contradiction. For after accepting to speak today in Hay-on-Wye in Raymond's memory, I discovered by an irony he himself would have relished that the lecture was to be given at a festival sponsored by the *Sunday Times*.

For some years now, this newspaper has gone to great pains, in its editorial columns, to inform what it calls the intelligentsia of the country that it is out of step with the – what is the word? – 'entrepreneurial' mood of the times, and that, by their insistence on values beyond the purely personal, artists and writers make themselves objects of contempt to the kind of people who are putting Britain back on her feet.

Well, for myself, I can only say these are fine times to be out of step with. Considering the ugliness and malice with which the newspaper has conducted its campaign, I wondered for a moment why the *Sunday Times*, with all its self-importance and power, had never actually succeeded in making me angry. And I realized it is a trick of my character only to be truly angry with those whom I hold in the highest regard. Hearing this newspaper planned to sponsor a literary festival, my first thought was not to wonder at their hypocrisy, but instead to think, 'Well, that's good. They want to make amends.' And I was grateful. It is a fact. From certain people we are grateful for anything. From others, great men, great women, we expect everything. May it always be so.

1989

2

THE PLAY IS IN THE AIR
On Political Theatre

To begin with the obvious: the playwright writes plays. He chooses plays as his way of speaking. If he could speak more clearly in a lecture, he would lecture; if polemic suited him, he'd be a journalist. But he chooses the theatre as the most subtle and complex way of addressing an audience he can find. Because of that, I used to turn down all invitations to speak in public, because I didn't want an audience to hear the tone of my voice. I don't like the idea that they can get a hand-down version of my plays sitting in a lecture hall and sizing me up. In the theatre I am saying complex and difficult things. I do not want them reduced either by my views on the world, or, more importantly, the audience's idea of my views. I want no preconceptions. I don't want, 'Oh, of course Hare is a well-known anti-vivisectionist, that's why there's that scene where the dog is disembowelled.' I want the dog cut up and the audience deciding for themselves if they like the sight or not. The first lesson the playwright learns is that he is not going to be able to control an audience's reactions anyway; if he writes an eloquent play about the sufferings of the Jews in the Warsaw Ghetto there is always going to be someone in the audience who comes out completely satisfied with the evening, saying at last someone's had the guts to say it, those Nazis knew what they were about. As you can't control people's reactions to your plays, your duty is also not to reduce people's reactions, not to give them easy handles with which they can pigeon-hole you, and come to comfortable terms with what you are saying.

So why, then, am I changing tack and beginning to try and speak a little in public about the theatre? It is partly because I have been trying in the last few months to put my ear to the ground and find out what a particular section of my audience is thinking and feeling; but it is also for other and very pressing reasons which I hope will become clear as I go on.

I'd like to start with a story which has always taken my breath away, from Hardy's incomparable novel *Jude the Obscure*. The young mother, homeless in Oxford, living in appalling poverty with a family she cannot possibly support, puts her head in her hands, and says in the presence of her eldest boy, 'O, it is better if we had never been born.' Later that day she goes upstairs.

At the back of the door were fixed two hooks for hanging garments, and from these the forms of [her] two youngest children were suspended, by a piece of box-cord round each of their necks, while from a nail a few yards off the body of little Jude was hanging in a similar manner. An overturned chair was near the eldest boy, and his glazed eyes were slanted into the room; but those of the girl and the baby were closed.

I always think this is the ultimate cautionary tale for playwrights. That someone will actually take you at your word. That you will whip yourself up into a fine frenzy of dramatic writing on stage, have your superbly played heroine step harrowingly to the front of the stage and cry out in despair, 'It is better that we had never been born,' and there will in fact be an answering shot from the back of the stalls and one of the customers will slump down dead having committed the sin of assuming that the playwright means what he says.

For this is an austere and demanding medium. It is a place

where the playwright's ultimate sincerity and good faith is going to be tested and judged in a way that no other medium demands. As soon as a word is spoken on stage it is tested. As soon as a line is put into the reconstruction of a particular event, it will be judged. In this way the theatre is the exact opposite art to journalism; the bad journalist may throw off a series of casual and half-baked propositions, ill-considered, dashed-off, entertainment pieces to put forward a point of view which may or may not amuse, which may or may not be lasting, which may or may not be true; but were he once to hear those same words spoken out loud in a theatre he would begin to feel that terrible chill of being collectively judged and what had seemed light and trenchant and witty would suddenly seem flip and arch and silly.

Judgement. Judgement is at the heart of the theatre. A man steps forward and informs the audience of his intention to lifelong fidelity to his wife, while his hand, even as he speaks, drifts at random to the body of another woman. The most basic dramatic situation you can imagine; the gap between what he says and what we see him to be opens up, and in that gap we see something that makes theatre unique; that it exposes the difference between what a man says and what he does. That is why nothing on stage is so exciting as a great lie; why *Brassneck* never recovers as a play after its greatest liar is killed off at the end of the first act.

I would suggest crudely that one of the reasons for the theatre's possible authority, and for its recent general drift towards politics, is its unique suitability to illustrating an age in which men's ideals and men's practice bear no relation to each other; in which the public profession of, for example, socialism has often been reduced by the passage of history to wearying personal fetish, or even chronic personality disorder. The theatre is the best way of showing the gap between what is said and what is seen to be done, and that is why, ragged and gap-toothed as it is, it has still a far healthier potential than some of the other, poorer, abandoned arts.

To explain what I mean I should tell you of a conversation I once had with a famous satirist of the early sixties who has been pushed further and further into the margin of the culture, later and later into the reaches of the night on BBC2, or Radio Solent, or wherever they still finally let him practise his art. He said, 'I don't understand why every day I feel my own increasing irrelevance to the country I am meant to be satirizing.' I suggested it is because satire depends upon ignorance. It is based on the proposition, 'If only you knew.' Thus the satirist can rail, 'If only you knew that Eden was on benzedrine throughout the Suez crisis, stoned out of his head and fancy-free; if only you knew that the crippled, stroke-raddled Churchill dribbled and farted in Cabinet for two years after a debilitating stroke, and nobody dared remove him; if only you knew that Cabinet Ministers sleep with tarts, that Tory MPs liaise with crooked architects and bent off-shore bankers: if only you knew.' But finally after his railing, the satirist may find that the audience replies, 'Well, we do know now; and we don't believe it will ever change. And knowing may well not affect what we think.'

This is the first stage of what I think Marxists call 'raising consciousness'; a worthy aim and yet ... consciousness has been raised in this country for a good many years now and we seem further from radical political change than at any time in my life. The traditional function of the radical artist – 'Look at those Borgias; look at this bureaucracy' – has been undermined. We have looked. We have seen. We have known. And we have not changed. A pervasive cynicism paralyses public life. And the once-active, early sixties' satirist is left on the street corner, peddling pathetic grubby little scraps of sketch and song – Callaghan's love life? Roy Jenkins' taste for claret . . .

And so we must ask, against this background, what can the playwright accomplish that the satirist cannot? What tools does he have that the satirist lacks?

The first question a political playwright addresses himself to is: why is it that in advanced industrial societies the record of revolutionary activity is so very miserable, so very, very low? The urban proletariat in this country knows better than we ever can that they are selling their labour to capital; many of them know far better than we of the degradations of capitalism. Of the wretched and the inadequate housing into which many of them are born; of the grotesque, ever worsening imbalance in the educational system whereby the chances of progress to examinability even at 'O' level, even at CSE level, are still ludicrously low; of the functional and enslaving work they are going to have to do; of the lack of control they are going to suffer at their own workplace. Of all these things they know far more than we, and, most importantly, they are familiar with socialist ideas which see their sufferings as part of a soluble political pattern.

Worse, we have lived through a time of economic depression, which classically in Marxist theory is supposed to throw up those critical moments at which the proletariat may seize power. And yet, in my own estimate, European countries have been more unstable during times of affluence than times of depression. It is hard to believe in the historical inevitability of something which has so frequently not happened, or rather, often been nearest to happening in places and circumstances furthest away from those predicted by the man who first suggested it.

Confronted by this apparent stasis, the English writer is inclined to answer with a stasis of his own, to sigh and imagine that the dialectic has completely packed in, or rather got stuck in some deep rift from which he cannot jump it out. And so he begins to lose faith in the possibility of movement at all. Compare this with a post-revolutionary society, like China, where the dialectic is actually seen to mean something in people's lives. In the play *Fanshen* it is dynamic. Political practice answers to theory and yet modifies it; the party answers to the people and is modified by it. The fight is for political structures which answer people's needs; and people themselves are changed by living out theoretical ideas. It is a story of change and progress.

Must it always be, however, that Marxist drama set in Europe reflects the state of revolutionary politics with an answering sluggishness of its own? By this, I mean that sinking of the heart when you go to a political play and find that the author really believes that certain questions have been answered even before the play has begun. Why do we so often have to endure the demeaning repetition of slogans which are seen not as transitional aids to understanding, but as ultimate solutions to men's problems? Why the insulting insistence in so much political theatre that a few gimcrack mottoes of the left will sort out the deep problems of reaction in modern England? Why the urge to caricature? Why the deadly stiffness of limb? Brecht uncoils the great sleeping length of his mind to give us, in everything but the greatest of his writing, exactly that impression, the god-like feeling that the questions have been answered before the play has begun. Even his idea of irony is insufferably coy. He parades it, he hangs it out to dry as if it were proof of the broadness of his mind. It should not need such demonstration.

I do understand the thinking. The Marxist playwright working in a fairly hostile medium feels that his first job is to declare his allegiance, to show his hand if you like. He thinks that because the play itself is part of the class struggle, he must first say which side he is on and make that clear, before he proceeds to lay out the ideas of the play as fairly as he may. To me this approach is rubbish, it insults the audience's intelligence; more important it insults their experience; most important it is also a fundamental misunderstanding of what a play is. A play is not actors, a play is not a text; a play is what happens between the stage and the audience. A play is a performance. So if a play is to be a weapon in the class struggle, then that weapon is not going to be the things you are saying; it is the interaction of what you are saying and what the audience is thinking. The play is in the air. The woman in the balcony who yelled out during the famous performance of *Othello*, 'Can't you see what he's going to do, you stupid black fool?' expressed the life of that play better than any writer I ever knew; and understood the nature of performance better than the slaves of Marxist fashion.

I think this fact, that we are dealing, all of us, actors, writers, directors, with something we cannot calibrate because it is in the air and nowhere else, accounts for the fact that theatre is often bound up in mysticism and why it is known throughout the Western world as a palace of boredom. Is there any boredom like boredom in the theatre? Is there anything as grey, as soul-rotting, as nerve-tearing, as being bored in the theatre, or as facing the bleak statistical likelihood that you will be bored in the theatre for 99 per cent of the time you spend there? I can sleep anywhere on earth, haystack, bus, railway station; I have slept soundly with mortar bombs landing eight hundred yards away, yet I cannot sleep in the theatre. This I put down to the fact that I cannot bear to sleep when so many of my fellow human beings are in such intolerable pain around me; not only my comrades in the audience, but also my colleagues on stage. For if theatre is judgement, it is also failure. It is failing, and failing, and failing.

I think that it is in some way to avoid this uncomfortable fact that dramatists have lately taken to brandishing their political credentials as frequently as possible throughout their work, and that political theatre groups have indulged in such appalling overkill, in some way to stave off failure with an audience; to flaunt your sincerity, to assert and re-assert a simple scaffolding of belief in order not to face the real and unpredictable dangers of a genuinely live performance is all a way of not being judged. It is understandable, but it is wrong. It is in no way as craven as the scaffolding you will find in West End theatres, the repeated reassurances to the audience that narrow lives are the only lives worth leading; nor in my mind is it in any way as poisonous as the upper-middle-brow, intellectual comedies which have become the snob fashion of the day, meretricious structures full of brand references to ideas at which people laugh in order to prove that they have heard of them; the pianola of chic which tinkles night and day in Shaftesbury Avenue, and which is thought to be real music in the smart Sunday papers. The English theatre loves the joker, the detached observer, the man who stands outside; no wonder, faced with this ubiquity of tat, that political theatre tends to be strident and unthinking, not in its attitude to its content, but in its distrust of the essential nature of performance itself.

Historically it is hard for a serious playwright to be confident. History has not behaved in the way that was asked of it; and the medium itself in which we work has chronic doubts about its own audibility. Bronowski hectors from a corner of a tenement slum; while the Queen settles down on Fridays to watch *It Ain't Half Hot Mum*. The airways are saturated with conflicting messages. All a playwright can do is promise to speak only when he has something to say; but when he speaks, what special role can he assume?

For five years I have been writing history plays. I try to show the English their history. I write tribal pieces, trying to show how people behaved on this island, off this continental shelf, in this century. How this Empire vanished, how these ideals died. Reading Angus Calder's *The People's War* changed a lot of my thinking as a writer; an account of the Second World War through the eyes of ordinary people, it attempts a complete alternative history to the phoney and corrupting history I was taught at school. Howard Brenton and I attempted in *Brassneck* to write what I have no doubt Calder would still write far better than we, an imagined subsequent volume *The People's Peace*, as seen, in our case, through the lives of the petty bourgeoisie, builders, solicitors, brewers, politicians, the masonic gang who carve up provincial England. It was my first step into the past. When I first wrote, I wrote in the present day, I believed in a purely contemporary drama; so as I headed backwards, I worried I was avoiding the real difficulties of the day. It took me time to realize that the reason was, if you write about now, just today and nothing else, then you seem to be confronting only stasis, but if you begin to describe the undulations of history, if you write plays that cover passages of time, then you begin to find a sense of movement, of social change, if you like; and the facile hopelessness that comes from confronting the day and only the day, the room and only the room, begins to disappear and in its place the writer can offer a record of movement and variance.

You will see what I am arguing. The Marxist writer spends a great deal of time rebuking societies for not behaving in the way that he expected them to; but also, furious because change is not taking the form he would like it to, he denigrates or ignores the real changes which have taken place in the last thirty years. A great empire falls apart, offering, as it collapses, a last great wash of wealth through this country, unearned, unpaid for, a shudder of plenty, which has dissolved so many of the rules which kept the game in order; while intellectuals grope wildly for an answer, any answer to the moral challenge of collectivism, the citizens have spent and spent, after the war in time of wealth, but recently in a time of encroaching impoverishment. We are living through a great, groaning, yawling festival of change – but because this is England it is not always seen on the streets. In my view it is seen in the extraordinary intensity of people's personal despair, and it is to that despair that as a historical writer I choose to address myself time and time again: in *Teeth 'n' Smiles*, in *Knuckle*, in *Plenty*.

I feel exactly as Tom Wolfe does in a marvellous account of his opportunities as a writer:

About the time I came to New York ... the most serious novelists abandoned the richest terrain of the novel: namely, society, the social tableau, manners and morals, the whole business of the 'way we live now'. There is no novelist who captures the sixties in America or even in New York in the same sense that Thackeray was the chronicler of London in the 1840s and Balzac was the chronicler of Paris and all of France ... That was marvellous for journalists, I tell you that. The sixties were one of the most extraordinary decades in American history in terms of manners and morals. Manners and morals *were* history in the sixties. I couldn't believe the scene I saw spread out before me. But what really amazed me as a writer I had it practically all to myself ... As fast as I could possibly do it, I was turning out articles on this amazing spectacle I saw bubbling and screaming right there ... and all the while I knew that some enterprising novelist was going to come along and *do* the whole marvellous scene in one gigantic bold stroke. It was so ready, so ripe – beckoning ... and it never happened.

I can't tell you how accurately that expresses a feeling I have always had as a playwright and which I know colleagues have experienced, that sense that the greater part of the culture is simply looking at the wrong things. I became a writer by default, to fill in the gaps, to work on the areas of the fresco which were simply ignored, or appropriated for the shallowest purposes: rock music, black propaganda, gun-selling, diplomacy. And yet I cannot believe to this day that a more talented writer will not come along and *do* the whole scene. In common with other writers who look with their own eyes, I have been abused in the newspapers for being hysterical, strident and obscene, when all I was doing was observing the passing scene, its stridency, its hysteria, its obscenity, and trying to put it in a historical context which the literary community seems pathologically incapable of contemplating. In *Teeth 'n' Smiles* a girl chooses to go to prison because it will give her an experience of suffering which is bound in her eyes to be more worthwhile than the life she could lead outside: not one English critic could bring himself to mention this central event in the play, its plausibility, its implications. It was beyond their scope to engage with such an idea. And yet, how many people here have close friends who have taken control of their own lives, only to destroy them?

We are drawing close, I think, to what I hope a playwright can do. He can put people's sufferings in a historical context; and by doing that, he can help to explain their pain. But what I mean by history will not be the mechanized absolving force theorists would like it to be; it will be those strange uneasy factors that make a place here and nowhere else, make a time now and no other time. A theatre which is exclusively personal, just a place of private psychology, is inclined to self-indulgence; a theatre which is just social is inclined to unreality, to the impatient blindness I've talked about today. Yeats said, out of our quarrel with others, we make rhetoric, while out of our quarrel with ourselves, we make poetry. I value both, and value the theatre as a place where both are given weight.

I write love stories. Most of my plays are that. Over and over again I have written about romantic love, because it never goes away. And the view of the world it provides, the dislocation it offers, is the most intense experience that many people know on earth.

And I write comedy because ... such ideas as the one I have just uttered make me laugh.

And I write about politics because the challenge of communism, in however debased and ugly a form, is to ask whether the criteria by which we have been brought up are right; whether what each of us experiences uniquely really is what makes us valuable; whether every man should really be his own cocktail; or whether our criteria could and should be collective, and if they were, whether we would be any happier. However absolute the sufferings of people in the totalitarian Soviet countries, however decadent the current life of the West, the fact is that this question has only just been asked, and we have not even the first hundredth of an answer. To give up now would be death.

I said at the beginning that I have chosen to speak, in part simply to find out, to put my ear to the ground. And I must tell you what I find in universities. I find a generation who are cowed, who seem to have given up on the possibility of change, who seem to think that most of the experiments you could make with the human spirit are likely to be doomed or at any rate highly embarrassing. There is a demeaning nostalgia for the radicalism of the late sixties, people wanting to know exactly what the Vietnam marches were like. To me it would be sad if a whole generation's lives were shaped by the fact that a belief in change had fallen temporarily out of fashion; in Tom Wolfe's terms, it would be sad if this historical period had no chronicler.

Our lives must be refreshed with images which are not official, not approved; that break what George Orwell called 'the Geneva conventions of the mind'. These images may come on television, something of a poisoned well in my view, because of its preference for censoring its own best work, or simply banning it; or they may come in this unique arena of judgement, the theatre.

I find it strange to theorize. Mostly theatre is hard work and nothing else. It is no coincidence that some of the British theatre's loudest theorists are notoriously incompetent inside a rehearsal room. It is a different kind of work. The patterns that I've made today in my own work and talking about others are purely retrospective, just the afterbirth; the wonder of performance is – you will always be surprised. The short, angry, sandy-haired, squat playwright turns out to write plays which *you* experience as slow, languorous, relaxed and elegant: the great night you had in the theatre two years ago turns out upon rereading to be a piece of stinking fish. I would wish it no other way.

An old American vaudevillian of the thirties drank his career away, fell into universal disfavour, but was finally found and put into an old people's home in California by a kindly producer who had once worked with him many years before. Visiting the old actor on his deathbed, the producer said, 'You are facing death. Is it as people describe? Is there a final sense of reassurance, a feeling of resignation, that sense of letting go that writers tell us consoles the dying?' 'Not at all,' said the comic, 'on the contrary. Death is none of those things that I was promised. It is ugly and fierce and degrading and violent. It is hard,' he said, 'hard as playing comedy.' All I would add is, not as hard as writing it.

1978

3
LOOKING FOOLISH
On Taking Risks

The retirement of Alan Hancox as a distinguished Director of the Cheltenham Festival provides me with the occasion to talk a little about my profession. The blurb on the Festival programme describes me, rather mysteriously and on no evidence that I can recall, as 'a writer who is not afraid of exposing himself'. I hope not too many of you have been lured here on the false promise of seeing me do anything but talk. It seems it would hardly be necessary. Talks by writers have taken the place of music hall in our popular culture. All summer long, P. D. James waves to Ruth Rendell as they pass each other on opposite lanes of Britain's motorways. In certain unstable developing countries it is illegal for more than thirty-five people to gather together *without* being addressed by Hanif Kureishi. Faced with the choice between going to your plays and listening to you talk, a fair proportion of the public will always prefer to suck you through a straw. But it's tricky. Pronouncements by playwrights on the general state of the theatre soften quickly, like bad fruit, into special pleading. Ambitiously titled polemics on Why We Need More Political Theatre or Why Expressionism Is a Good Thing turn out to be essays whose inevitable purpose is to explain why the playwright thinks his or her plays are set on a better course than other people's. If my gift were for farce, then I am sure, having finished my latest play, I would find myself explaining why Farce is the Highest Art; if my flair were for the psychological, then no doubt I would prefer to knock off fifteen hundred words on why only by searching inside people's minds can the theatre renew itself.

In Tolstoy's great novel *Resurrection*, the Count is shocked and astonished to find that a prostitute is not ashamed of her work, until of course he realizes that we all, however lowly, take care to surround ourselves with people and ideas which reassure us that our work has worth. When our leading classical directors move onto assembling crowd-pleasing musicals for the West End and Broadway, then they argue righteously for what they then prefer to call Popular Theatre; when my own play closes in ten days, then I rediscover, with a special urgency, the unique importance of that old theatrical alibi, the Right To Fail. After the Fact comes the Theory. After the Parade, your mind gets out its brushes and begins to sweep the road.

You will do well then to regard what I have to say with a certain caution, for it is essentially the *a posteriori* reasoning of someone who has no option but to write for the theatre. I am sure Salman Rushdie is in good faith when he argues that in a secular age the novel can in some way take over the function of religion. But I am also sure that he is swayed in his mind by the fact that he himself is – hey presto! – a novelist. Like most writers, I did not choose my profession. It chose me. As a young man, I discovered in myself, almost by accident, a facility for writing dialogue. Although it did not take me long to realize that a gift for dialogue qualifies you to be a playwright no more than a gift for mixing sand and water qualifies you to build cathedrals, I was glad at least, finally, to be good at something. (I loved cricket, but had never made more than twenty-nine runs.) Yet even after stumbling on this discovery, my idea of my own abilities was confined by the circumstances of belonging to a particular and talented generation. My friend Christopher Hampton had a play in the West End when he was nineteen. So when my own first play was premièred when I was twenty-three, I felt I was limping into London long past my reasonable sell-by date. Both Howard Brenton and Trevor Griffiths seemed to glow with a vocational confidence which I entirely lacked.

The great mercy of the profession that I did end up in is that it does not allow for what is usually called a career. It is in the nature of the job that nothing can be planned. Each time you start, you start afresh. Experience may come to guide you more reliably in the tailoring of a play. It will certainly help with the pockets and cuffs. But the particular need to write, the special urgency which demands that you address this subject and no other, cannot be commanded at will. Like sexual desire, it rises unbidden. Unless the play comes from some secret place inside yourself, what chance can it have of reaching that same place inside the audience?

It is important I stress at the outset the privacy of the impulse which makes most of us write, for it is, to me, now the only proper starting point for any discussion about what the theatre can and cannot do. It explains why, in a lot of contemporary commentary on plays and films, there is often a certain exasperation in the writer's tone. Outsiders, sitting on the sidelines and surveying the stuff they are offered, seem puzzled by how playwrights make their choices. Commentators write as if they cannot understand why these stubborn people do not turn their attention from the trivial subject matter which happens to compel them to material which the critic regards as infinitely more important. The ability to write is assumed to be a technical facility, a skill, like engineering, which for some reason is usually being negligently applied to the wrong areas of life. Why, they ask, are there not more plays about AIDS? Or unemployment? Or the housing shortage? Those of us who are drawn to public subject matter have the charge pressed against us more directly. Political writers are treated as short-order chefs, who ought to be able to go à la carte. Because I have written plays about the Chinese revolution, the death of rock and roll, and the Church of England, it is assumed that but for my own intransigence I could turn with equal expertise to cooking up plays on Central America, satellite television and the Hare Krishna movement.

This critical desire to set a writer's agenda for him or her, though understandable, is in fact as vulgar as the request I once received from the producers of *Agatha*, who asked me to write the last scene of their film for them – the last scene only, please note – on the grounds that it was set on a train. 'And, David, you're very good at train scenes.' It is always necessary to explain in any such discussion that most of us – except for the gifted few – write only what we can. We write to the best of our ability. And we are lost to explain what draws us to one place, and not to another; or why the invention of one character animates us, while another dulls our mind. At no time are we more conscious of this unreason than when we allocate fates to the people we have created. We shoot them, or marry them, we promote them or divorce them, we fulfil them or condemn them to a life of utter loneliness. An impulse which is certainly not justice takes over, and we do what feels right. Challenged afterwards, we may talk clearly about what we have written. But most of us can say very little about why.

And yet. Standing aside from the process for a moment, I can at least recognize, if not sympathize with, the disappointment which motivates critics into the foolishness of asking writers to write differently. They have in a sense been spoilt.

Since 1956 it has been the expectation of every British theatre-goer that there will be, if not a stream, at least a steady trickle of plays which address themselves to the contemporary world. Although in a hundred countries, including the United States, such an assumption would be an absurdity, here in Britain the expectation has persisted. However, since the late seventies, good new plays seem to have been harder to come by. Opera and the novel have, in a certain literary class, enjoyed an ascendancy, both inside and outside London, without ever taking over the role forged for the theatre by John Osborne, Joan Littlewood and others of offering a place where the recognizable thoughts and feelings of the time may seem to echo and illuminate its social history.

I have two children, both aged eleven, who have never lived under any other Prime Minister but Thatcher. Recently, in what I hope we may come to know as the late years of her premiership, I have been asked two questions with increasing frequency, and often by the same person, who seems not to understand that they are, on the surface at least, mutually contradictory. Do I not think, I am always asked, that given the massive changes both in Britain and in Europe in the last decade overtly political theatre has lost a great deal of its clout? And then, in the same breath, aren't I worried that we may soon lose Mrs Thatcher, because then, surely, contemporary playwrights will have nothing left to write about?

Before trying to disentangle these two questions and say something of what I do see in the subtle relationship between a country's artistic life and its politics, let me first draw attention to the generalized millennialism which lies behind the way many people are now thinking. The Berlin Wall has been breached, and it is agreed to be an event of great significance, though wherein exactly that significance lies not everyone is absolutely agreed. In the minds of certain right-wing newspaper editors it represents the definitive triumph of what is called the free market over the obvious evils of communism. The plays of Bertolt Brecht have been declared by the *Daily Telegraph* to be the most conspicuous casualties of this victory, because they raise questions which, in the *Telegraph*'s view, are no longer relevant. The corollary of this thinking is a fashionable prejudice which sees writing as an opportunist activity. Writers who wish to do anything other than mildly amuse are seen as parasites, ungratefully cashing in on the few and occasional shortcomings of a vastly superior system, instead of celebrating the freedom of a society which has delivered them their physical well-being. It is seen as a moral issue. Writers *ought* to say thank you. The government has been generous enough to provide writers and film-makers with all the images of public squalor and deprivation from which they make their fat livings. It is irresponsible of them not to pay tribute to the ideology which has delivered them their own prosperity.

You will forgive me if I do not pause long to deal with this argument. Freedom is not a privilege. It is a right. Just as twenty-five years ago nobody but journalists or politicians used the awful phrase 'the permissive society' for the simple reason that nobody else could see why there had to be any permitting in the first place, or indeed who it was who was meant to *do* the permitting, so now it is necessary to remind governments that their job is not to grant freedoms, but to protect and administer them on behalf of the people to whom they properly belong. I am sure it is irritating to governments that artists do not always take the same benign view of things as they do. I am sure it was once irritating to the governments of Russia and Czechoslovakia. But could anything be more insulting to our friends in Eastern Europe who have struggled so hard for their freedoms than to tell them that in the West there are people who would prefer them not to exercise those freedoms, for fear it shows ingratitude to our rulers?

Behind this attempt to blackmail writers into loving Western governments lies the extraordinary notion that once an artist has meat and potatoes on his plate, his job is then to fall into line. He will then be expected to produce versions of pastoral. I was very shocked once, visiting the Royal College of Music, where the general level of education appeared to be extremely rudimentary, to find that large numbers of students believed that great suffering was the only guarantee of great art. They also believed that racial or political persecution provided the handiest way of securing that necessary suffering. It was their view that the century's greatest music had been written in Russia under Stalin, and that Shostakovich was the century's greatest composer because, explicitly, history had handed him the century's worst deal. There was, in the way a number of students spoke, a corresponding fatalism about the chances of attempting to compose decent music in the West. Great feeling was not possible because we did not live in a society which forced it from us. There was, they felt, nothing for them to write about, because they lived in such an essentially comfortable bourgeois democracy, and in such places the need for art could not be very strong.

It seems to me it has to be an article of faith among us – for why else would we write willingly? – that writers are not horses, who need to be kicked in the flanks by history at five-minute intervals. Without the spur, without blood below the saddle, Dickens, Jane Austen and that notorious bourgeois, William Shakespeare, produced work quite as valuable and profound as those who, like Lorca and Gorky, became history's most eminent literary victims. Exciting times neither guarantee nor preclude great art. Recently, we have heard actors in East German theatres complain that their work is no longer prized. They say that when their society was in chains, then people flocked to the theatre because it was a place where, under the cover of metaphor, the audience could bask in a vision of life dramatically different from the one they then led. Everything was, in a sense, pre-charged. The audience came and, before the curtain even went up, began to provide the energy which would make the evening spark. But in complaining that those days are now gone, and that the once-eager audience has fled to buy Reeboks and eat in McDonalds on Kurfürstendamm, the East German actors do not prove to me that the need itself for art has died; only that the audience's recognition of that need is less automatic than it once was.

No one can deny that in the West that need does often seem to be sleeping. But by the use of surprise, the theatre may always re-awaken it. For, above all, the theatre is the place to go for something you do not expect. For this reason, it is the only major literary form in which nobody ever writes sequels. The whole point of the theatre is that we never wish to meet the same characters twice. When, by legend, Shakespeare was prevailed on to bring Falstaff back, he brought back someone with the same characteristics, but none of the original genius. Just as we, the writers, sit down at the paper each time and start afresh, so too the audience only remembers its forgotten needs if it, too, has started afresh. It is the theatre's aim to draw forth from people some of their most private and intimate emotions. But – and here is its governing paradox – it asks of its audience that these most private feelings be summoned up in a public place.

Of a certain French film an American critic once wrote that her readers should beware whom they took as their companions to see it. Its virtues were so special and particular that you felt they might be damaged if the person next to you were not on the same wavelength. To be with the wrong person would be to spoil the film. Similarly, a friend of mine confessed that she had wished she had gone to a certain play of mine alone. Of course she was fond of the man she was with, but she did not want her own response to the evening spoilt by anything so crude as the glass of acidic white wine and the inevitable what-do-you-think-of-it-so-far in the interval. She hated the sound of the audience's laughter, because it seemed to be bullying her. It spoilt the illusion that the play was there to speak to her and her alone. When actors complain that a particular audience is good or bad, according to the enthusiasm they show at particular lines, or the brightness of their eyes at the curtain call, then it is wise to remind them that there are evenings – Saturday nights are the worst – where a so-called 'good' audience will laugh itself out of a play in the first half-hour and go home depressed; and there are other so-called 'bad' nights when the torpid audience does not seem to stir, and yet when the play is, unknown to the actors, offering maybe just two or three people the most important theatre-going night of their lives.

It is this I love in the theatre. I love its volatility. Its special beauty seems to me to come from the fact that at seven-thirty you have no idea how you will be feeling at ten-fifteen. And at ten-fifteen you will look back, as across an ocean, to the almost unrecognizable stranger who arrived at seven-thirty. If you object that this definition of what is best about the theatre might equally well apply to attending a good cock-fight, or for that matter to spending a long evening in a pub, then I will admit that I was for a long time haunted by a remark made by Bill Cotton (not he of 'Wakey-wakey!' but his equally eminent son), who, when controller of BBC Television, observed that he could see no real need for plays in his schedules, for no play had yet been written which matched the intensity and excitement of the 1966 England–West Germany World Cup Final. That, he said, was real drama. It has taken me over twenty years to work out how wrong he was, and in what way. But at the end I come down to suggesting he misses the two distinctive virtues of real plays: they show us that feelings which we had thought private turn out to be common ground with others, and, uniquely, they appeal as much to our heads as to our hearts. Or, rather, they send our minds and hearts spinning together, so that we cannot tell which is which.

I explained earlier that I believed good writing was un-forced, that it came not just by the application of conscious effort, but from some spontaneous source inside ourselves; and now I would also insist on the converse, that a play only moves us as an audience when our response to it is also unforced. As soon as we feel we are being got at, the play dies. It is for this reason that I do not share the fashionable excitement about the revival of the musical, nor am I much taken with the sudden popularity of opera. Almost inevitably, except in the greatest hands, they are forms in which it is clear exactly what we are meant to feel and when. We are pro-grammed to respond when the so-called 'great tune' comes round, as it invariably does, like Christmas, or a paralysingly boring relative, for the fifth time in the evening. Oddly, of all feelings, hysteria is one of the easiest to create in a theatre. You may do it as easily in a playhouse as you may on the tube. Tub-thumping big tunes and flag-waving, revolving sets and huge, menacing choruses who come marching down towards the footlights, are the theatrical equivalent of shouting 'fire' on the underground. They undeniably have an effect. And yet, to me, because they make us conscious that our response is already expected, because we are asked to feel things on demand, they have no real life. The stage clears. The fat lady is left alone. Here comes the aria. Here comes high C. No one can be human and fail to realize that their emotional make-up consists, in part, of a series of buttons waiting to be pressed. But, speaking for myself, I would rather not sight the big, grubby thumb of showbusiness bearing down on my buttons from too far away.

Of course those who hate the theatre will object that all this is a matter of degree, that musicals only do blatantly what less popular plays do by stealth. By its very nature, they claim, there cannot be a public performance which does not depend on manipulation. Only in the pure one-to-one relationship of poetry or the novel may a writer speak to a single person without distortion. And, in a sense, they are right. Any playwright learns early on the dangers and attractions of playing to the gallery. People behave differently when gathered together. To give a trivial example, for reasons no playwright can ever fathom, the mention of certain place-names will reduce any English audience to helpless laughter. It is enough merely to mention that a certain character comes from East Grinstead to provoke mass merriment. And there are regional variations to be mastered. In Nottingham, a place I happen to know, you may guarantee to detonate the house by mentioning that another character aspires to live in West Bridgeford. In all sorts of subtle and less obvious ways, you begin to sense what it is an audience likes to hear, and you learn how to pitch a play into the heart of their expectations. But the only healthy thing to do, having acquired this knowledge, is at once to mislay it.

Anyone not sufficiently horrified by the dangers of calculating his or her effects should be chastened by the example of the American cinema, where a great tradition of genuine story-telling has now been reduced to the endless replaying of the same factory-line emotional triggers, which are set, like charges, to go off at five-minute intervals in Hollywood films.

Dogs are patted, children are hugged, wives are kissed on the cheek, not in any way to convince us that this is real life, but purely to offer us a package of feel-good moments, whose unspoken aim is to convince us that the leading man is a thoroughly nice person, and that good people live in a thoroughly nice world. It was always objected to the old Hollywood that it created a fantasy world of make-believe. But fifty years ago the strength of the actors and the complexity of the stories corresponded strangely with the audience's inner landscape. Now story-telling has been reduced to signalling. People are nice or nasty. Things happen, not for their own sake, but for the effect they are sure to have on us. A gun is produced, to make us feel fear. A wife is produced, to make us feel safe. The true subject of the film becomes not the events it describes, but us, and our reactions, and most especially the three or four pounds with which we arrive, but which we no longer have when we depart. Shoot-outs, car-chases, funny little chaps who turn up from outer space with funny voices are all part of a huge Pavlovian carnival, whose chief purpose is to confirm in us all the feelings of self-esteem with which we arrive.

It is too easy to call such work cynical, for let no one doubt that bad art may involve just as much sincerity, industry and skill as good. No one contemplating the vast machinery of global show business could fail to be impressed by how much of this deliberately manipulative work, with its recurrent images of family and violence, is brilliantly designed, brilliantly photographed and even – though less frequently – brilliantly acted. But in its dependence on ready-made emotional responses, it seems to me to lack the one thing which makes public art exciting: it lacks risk.

I have called this lecture 'Looking Foolish' because I do not think anyone should embark on a life in the theatre or film unless they are in love with risk. If you are not to use the easy hand-holds, if your mind is on the thing itself and not on calculating your effects, then you must be willing to go out there in a way no other writer will have to, and make a painful fool of yourself. The novelist writes a book, finishes it, sends it to the editor, says to the reader 'There it is, I've done it, it's yours. Make of it what you will. But I shan't be around to find out.' At the most profound level, he or she remains undisturbed, wrapped in whatever impulse it was made him or her write the book, not having to subject that impulse to the scrutiny of six hundred people, all sitting there waiting to tell the author if he is talking out of his hat. If he sees a single reader on a train, then he goes into an ecstasy of embarrassment or excitement. Kingsley Amis once memorably complained that the great shortcoming of radio as a medium was that when you turned Frank Sinatra off, Frank Sinatra did not know. But the medium Kingsley Amis works in is just as unsatisfactory. If I throw Kingsley Amis' latest novel across the room, however resounding the thud, Kingsley Amis does not know. Alone, the playwright knows. He knows by the endurance of a thousand nights. He knows not just which play his audience warms to or distrusts, but which character, which sentiment, which scene, which line.

At my first play, a group of people, properly revolted by the sight of one actress sucking another actress's toes, got up to leave in the second scene. But, not pleased with the noise their seats made when they tipped them back, they then pushed them down again and forcibly re-flipped them so that they might make a more satisfying noise. I *heard*. And I have gone on hearing in every play I have written. I heard the man who turned at the end of the first act of a play of mine at the Bristol Old Vic and said to his companion, 'If this was on TV, I'd turn it off.' I heard the woman who put her arm consolingly round her boyfriend as they walked away from the theatre and said, 'I'm sorry, I'm sorry, darling, that was *my* idea.' I have heard the hacking coughs and the rustling sweet papers. I have watched the restless bottoms and the darting eyes. I have even seen one man shaken awake by his wife when his snoring threatened to drown out my whole play. But, more important, I have heard lines which I thought telling and funny being received in indifferent silence, while others assume a significance I never realized or intended. Characters I had intended as throwaways I have seen them take to their hearts, while they threw away the ones I loved. As I sought to surprise them, so, endlessly, the audience has surprised me. The experience of this, the direct experience of people's response to my work, makes me not a better writer than a poet or novelist of my same temperament and ability, nor even, God knows, a wiser one. But it makes me a different *kind* of writer. It makes me one who is at home with risk. It makes me unafraid of being passionate.

For – yes – it was my great good fortune in life to grow up in an era when people were not frightened to make fools of themselves. The ludicrous clothes of the sixties, the insane hairstyles, the pretentious babblings, the gurus, the guitars and the granny-glasses all expressed the artless, cheerful hopes of a generation who did not mind being seen to be idiots. The theatre prospered through my adolescence, as it had in the fifties, when writers like Osborne were not frightened that the power of their passions would sound silly on the stage. Now caution and carefulness rule everywhere. A breed of male British novelists has since appeared, whose distinctive aim is not to be caught out in the messy, embarrassing business of believing in anything. Ghastly late-night arts programmes on supposedly cultural channels, introduced by men in suits with shoulders a mile wide and sneers even wider, are there to tell us that style is infinitely more important than substance, that trash is more fun than humour, and that we do well to spend our time watching funky documentaries on the design history of the teaspoon. In their desperate eagerness to make culture hip, they drawl out sentences on plays and films with a weary sense of endgame, as if there were no chance of anything new being said, in a tone which is always sceptical, always knowing. The insistent, implicit message of the print and visual media is that the effort of changing anything is not worth making. The same millennialism which declares that capitalism has won its definitive victory over communism tries to tell us that human society is now arranged in the way it must be arranged for the rest of time, and that further comment is superfluous. Journalists who would once have dashed off to become foreign correspondents now stay at home to take up jobs as restaurant reviewers. Young actors who would once have rushed to join fringe groups which tried at least to show the audience what was happening in their own lives, now stand on steeply raked stages with scenery at crazy angles, performing obscure minor classics, shouting a lot, because critics and directors have persuaded them that over-acting is somehow more European.

Proust tells us that it is characteristic of all men to believe that they have lived through a period of great changes; and yet, characteristically, they also believe there will not be any more. Having finally adapted to the invention of the telephone, they profess astonishment when the aeroplane arrives. In our own age people are encouraged by politicians to build up money and possessions, not for the pleasures they bring, but like sandbags, to provide the illusion of permanence. But however well we hedge ourselves in, great art arrives with the repeated, bittersweet message: this will not last. Novels and poems, by their nature, are built to defy time. They aspire to be things which survive, in spite of the odds. Theatre alone revels in impermanence. Like us, it is there and then it is gone. Understanding this better than anyone, our greatest national playwright has certain favourite themes to which he returns. Power must be exercised and acknowledged, lest worse men take it from us. Like it or not, young men must grow up and assume the responsibilities of their fathers. Yet above and beyond these themes, through the dazzling span of his writing life, he returns again and again to one recurrent image: of the theatre, the 'insubstantial pageant' in its very brevity, in its very transience, beautifully resembling life itself.

Of all Oscar Wilde's exquisite jokes, the one I love best is when he was asked on the first night of his new play whether he thought it was going to be a success. 'The play', he replied, 'is already a success. Only the audience is in doubt.' It is a joke flung in the face of theatre itself, for the author of *Lady Windermere's Fan* and *The Importance of Being Earnest* knew full well that nothing is real, nothing exists in the theatre until the audience arrives. However deft or clever the play may look on the page, it cannot begin to release its power until the subtle process begins whereby the audience tests its perceptions against those of the author and the actors. In that testing process, both sides learn. Now that professional politicians no longer dare hold public meetings for fear of hearing what the electorate thinks, and now the Prime Minister, locked behind high gates, does not dare approach us, except through the mediation of television and advertising men, the theatre remains, in its ideal form, one of the few places where people of dissimilar views and backgrounds may come together and, in their shared response to what they see, find what they do and do not hold in common. I would define a good play as one which enables these acts of discovery. A good play, in the truest sense, ventilates democracy.

I said at the outset I would try to explain a little what I take to be the relationship between politics and the theatre. In thinking about these things, I have always felt great sympathy with a certain US Senator who in the early sixties when John Kennedy was hell-bent on bringing culture to the White House was quoted as saying: 'I know the President is telling us we should be listening to all these cellists and novelists, but I wish just one of them had some experience of getting an amendment onto a bill on the floor of the House.' The Senator seems to me to articulate a great truth: that writing is one thing, and running a country is another. The coincidence of a playwright–President in one Eastern European country has led to all sorts of fuzzy speculation that we may be entering some new age, in which writers will have a role in the state. But the history of writers' direct involvement in practical politics has hardly been happy. The surprise, to me, is not that Gorky falls out with Lenin, but that Gorky ever imagined he could work alongside Lenin in the first place. Just as I am far from convinced of Salman Rushdie's argument that, in an agnostic age, novelists form a sort of priesthood-in-waiting, so am I completely unpersuaded that, in an age of despair for conventional political parties, writers form a sort of government-in-waiting. It is simply not true. As a citizen I may have my own political allegiance. As a writer, I may regard politics as a subject which grown-up theatre should comprehend, and sicken of those who want the theatre just to be a play-pen for the psyche. But never for a moment do I suffer the illusion that a writer and a politician want the same things. Any writer who has ever been called in to help draft a manifesto, or re-phrase a pamphlet or speech, will know that our methods are different. One side wants to serve

53

what it calls the cause, the other what it likes to call the truth. Writers, absolutists by nature, can't help wanting to get things absolutely right. The politician's case against the writer will be that the absolute and utter truth is fine in principle, but it doesn't always help in getting the job done. The politician wants to achieve something. To this end, he must push his cause through. The writer's case against him is that he is often willing to cut corners. He is not always as fastidious with the truth as he might be.

This rift between thinkers and doers, like the unacknowledged rift in most societies between what should and can be done, goes back as far as time. It is better to acknowledge it, to accept that we do things different ways and to live on either riverbank than to splash around and get drowned in the middle. The politician will always complain that it is easy for a writer to sit in the grandstand and criticize the way the game is played. The writer will complain that the sacrifice of principle most politicians make effectively prevents them from achieving what they set out to do. I know writers always sound insufferably smug when they sit back and assert that their job is only to raise questions and not to answer them. But, in good part, it is true. And once you become committed to one particular answer, your freedom to ask new questions is seriously impaired.

To say this is not to despair of political theatre, but, on the contrary, to liberate it, to give it hope in an age in which the facile, dishonest millennialism of the right tries to tell us that questions of social justice have been settled for all time. We live in a country in which there has raged for twenty years a civil war of whose ending we have given up any hope, in which our methods of dealing with physical pain and mental illness are strained to near breaking point, in which the poorest tenth of us have been effectively abandoned by the representatives of the majority, in which our educational system has become the demoralized laughing-stock of Europe, and in which our legal system is so fundamentally misdirected that it takes fifteen years to admit its own most disastrous mistakes. We live among politicians who have neither the will nor the imagination to devise ways of helping the vast majority of the world's population who are still born into poverty and squalor. Who can truly look at this state of affairs and conclude that we have evolved the most perfect possible system of ordering our lives?

Things change. For better or worse, things go on changing. The job of the theatre is not to trap the audience in a stale political rhetoric which will be dead in ten days, but to liberate them from it by showing human beings who are more than slogans, who are seen and felt to be so much more than the nonsense that sometimes comes out of our mouths. On all writers – left and right, comic and serious, commercial and uncommercial – there is only one overriding and continuous pressure, and that is to make us show things as being simpler than they are. Interest groups will always be waiting, whether they are political, religious or aesthetic, none of them really interested in the work itself, but only in ambushing it for the signals they decide it gives off towards their special point of view. But a play is not a speech. A play is not a message. Least of all is a play a point of view. What is Shakespeare's point of view? What is Chekhov's? Sometimes we seem to know Ibsen's, then in the next play it seems to be the opposite. Does Ibsen say we must all tell the truth at all costs, or does he say the price of telling the truth is too high? To be honest, I'm damned if I remember. Which *is* his theme? That we can never escape our pasts? Or – hold on – does he insist that we must? And O'Neill ... Now what does O'Neill say? Does O'Neill say that people are better off living in the comfort of their illusions? Or does he say it's vital we destroy our illusions? I know it's one of these. Or, more likely, it's both. Great plays weave around their ideas, dart in and out of them, giving those ideas voluptuous expression, allowing us to discover where our own feelings lie, and then challenging us to move them. Ibsen, like any sane man or woman, knew both the attractions and dangers of telling the truth. He knew the truth-teller may become a hero, or a prig. Would we really think more of him if he always commanded us that one course of action was invariably right?

For plays are not their conclusions. Plays are their texture as well. If I am to answer my most frequently asked question – do I secretly fear Mrs Thatcher's fall from power, because it will deprive me of such a delicious source of subject matter? – then I must say no. No, as a citizen, it goes without saying, but also no, as a writer. I do not fear it. I will rejoice in it. For, as I have sought to explain today, Thatcherism appears to be in the fabric of my plays not because I put it there deliberately, but because it cannot help but be there. I am lost to understand how you write accurately about people's lives in Britain in the 1980s without the subject of materialism somehow seeping into the action, any more than you can write about South Africa without the subject of apartheid hanging in the air. A political author is, no more, no less than one who acknowledges this fact. An apolitical author is one who denies it.

To the second question – has political theatre lost some of its clout? – I am afraid I must offer a harsher and less popular answer. The answer is, if so, it is most likely the fault of those of us who are lucky enough to be performed and no one else. It is most probably because we do not write well enough. I am not sure this is down to the temper of the times. After twenty years, I am of course saddened by all those talented men and women who have given up on the theatre, either because they decided it could not deliver those changes which once inspired them to work in it, or else because they themselves grew to prefer another, less ulcerous way of life. But those of us remaining resort far too easily to the complaint that we are not understood. It is, after all, our job to make ourselves understood. We have every right to complain of what is written of us in newspapers, for there we are dependent on intermediaries whose values and attitudes may be entirely different from ours, and who can spoil our chances of reaching our potential audience. But of the audience itself – no – I truly believe we have *no* right to complain. It is our fault, not theirs, if we do not reach them with the things we have to say.

I entered just now one reservation when I noted this unforgiving attitude of mine applies only to those of us who are lucky enough to be performed. For, unless you are performed, how do you know? 'Most things', said Philip Larkin, 'are never meant.' No one, I am sure, sat down to dismember the British repertory movement. No one sent out orders to make sure that the arithmetic of running theatres outside London would no longer make sense. But, nationwide, we see the continuing, debilitating effects of artistic directors not being free to offer the programme of plays they would wish. The much-advertised 'right to fail' is really only the offspring of a much more important, much deeper right which is at the heart of the form itself: that is, the right to take risks. You cannot have theatre without risk. By its nature, it *is* risk. In the battle to attract sponsors who want an immediate return for their money and in aiming for failsafe commercial rewards, directors have, verifiably, junked living writers who embody exactly the dangers which make theatre exciting.

It is impossible to prove to any government that the theatre matters. And anything I might have to say on the subject will, I'm afraid, be countered by what we might, in chess terms, call the Mandy Rice-Davies defence: 'Well, he would say that, wouldn't he?' Governments may be presented with all sorts of unanswerable arguments – economic, educational, social – but finally they must back the survival of the performing arts on little more than a hunch, an instinct even, that there must be more to life than appears on the surface. Nothing has been odder in public life in the last decade than that strange magnetic impulse which drew Mrs Thatcher to address the General Assembly of the Church of Scotland. In talking about God, who admittedly turned out to have created the world according to principles remarkably congenial to the authors of the Conservative Party manifesto, she reminded me most of those people who insist on making jokes all the time, because they fear they have no sense of humour. She had the air of someone who was sick of being told they had no spiritual dimension, and who was therefore set, with gritted teeth, on proving otherwise. Implicit in her appearance, I am sure, was a tacit admission that the savage materialism she had preached over the previous years was as unsatisfying to her as to everyone else. Nothing else can explain all her subsequent obsession with the family and family morality, which, in the light of her own wrenching social policies, would otherwise be seen only as the crudest and most cynical hypocrisy.

To this obscure sense in her, and in her government, which sadly has the power to maintain or destroy the theatre outside London, I can only direct Freud's words: 'Art exists to reconcile men to the sacrifices they have made on civilization's behalf.' On the journey from being animal, something got lost. We miss it. I believe we need it. But I can never prove it. No one can.

*

Let me conclude, with pleasing symmetry, that just as it is the Festival Director's retirement which draws me here today, so what frightens me most in the theatre now is not so much the absence of young writers as the absence of young producers. The ones who have done most for new writing are now well into their forties. The novelist does not need to imagine the binding. The painter does not need to fantasize the gallery. But because theatre is a public form, there is barely a play-wright who is not helped by the certainty that his or her play will indeed go on, and in a particular place, and through the taste of a particular person. Nearly all the best modern writers – Athol Fugard, Caryl Churchill, Arthur Miller, David Mamet – are, or have been, identified with particular play-houses and particular men or women for whom they wanted to write. Even Samuel Beckett, apparently that most isolated of playwrights, acknowledged George Devine as 'the great inspirer'. For some reason, a playwright's juices flow best when they know that, waiting at the end of the long progress of the manuscript, is a person who will be loyal to them, whether they have written well or badly, and for whose opinion they cannot wait. Asked the greatest good fortune of my writing life, I would say it was to have known three or four such people. All a playwright needs is one person to believe in him, someone it's *worth* delivering a play to. You will know by now why I believe it's so essential. Finally, it's a way of sharing the risk.

1990

4

TIME OF UNEASE
At the Royal Court Theatre

I first went to work at the Court in the terrible wet November fogs of 1968. I had started a small travelling group called Portable Theatre and was living off my tiny one-tenth share of the gate. Christopher Hampton, fearing I would not survive the winter (he had visited my flat and invoked Gorky to describe how I lived), suggested that I start to read scripts, and within two months I took over from him as literary manager, there being no particular competition for the job because the wage was £7 10s a week.

I shared the same misconceptions many people had, that the Royal Court would be a political theatre, which it wasn't, and a writers' theatre, which it only rarely was. And it took me a long time to understand what its virtues were, partly because I found the people who worked there so strange. It's hard to remember now, but George Devine's famous remark that you had to choose your theatre as you would your religion did mean something then, and the body of people who worked at the Court were fiercely partisan about it, though quite what the exact tenets of the religion were, was, for an outsider, often fairly hard to grasp. I could see what everyone was against, because I was usually against it too – the hysterical torture of Shakespeare's texts at the RSC, or the absurd degrading comedies we had to endure in the West End – but when it came to defining what we were *for*, well, it was harder. It was almost a faith.

The faith had been tempered in adversity, a fact which, again, people now barely recall. Nobody's work in the English theatre since 1945 had been so misrepresented as William Gaskill's at the Court. A small group of loyalists had ridden out the storm, and in all the important things had been proved right: the austere bare-stage style of the productions would all too soon be the dominant staging cliché of the day, and Edward Bond in particular was coming to be valued, not as the sadistic maniac of the critics' imagination, but as one of the original writers of his time. But the psychological cost of surviving the constant critical abuse had been very great: the staff were arrogant, touchy, entrenched. And a boy from university, as I was, floating in, scarred from no battles, having seen nothing of the fight, found their prickliness incomprehensible. In a way I was destined never to get on.

I do remember those years as a time of almost perpetual unease, as I had one fight after another in the place. Every project had to be lobbied for by a medieval series of trials, which became more complex and severe in 1969 when a triumvirate of directors – Lindsay Anderson, William Gaskill and Anthony Page – took over the theatre, and developed an attitude to new work which made the championship of new scripts so arduous and humiliating that it's a wonder people stuck their necks out at all. No, they did not want plays from Howard Brenton (one artistic director said he should be taken out and buried in a hole in a field); yes, they *had* promised unconditionally and irrevocably that as an act of faith in the seven writers involved (Howard Brenton, Brian Clark, Trevor Griffiths, myself, Stephen Poliakoff, Hugh Stoddart, Snoo Wilson) *Lay-By* could be scheduled for a Sunday night performance, but now they had decided to *read* it and it was no longer a good idea; yes, I was now resident dramatist, but not for a moment should I take that to mean that they had any intention of doing my plays. (All resident dramatists in this period had their plays rejected; it became a feature of the job.)

I resigned a couple of times and was once farcically sacked for leaving in the interval of a particularly dreadful production, because, they said, it was letting the side down (there were more appeals to public school sentiment at the Court than in any institution I have known). But when I went to collect my wages nobody had remembered to stop them, so I simply went on appearing and nobody mentioned the matter again. I was often out of step with their taste, and yet, out of an odd mixture of resentment and respect, I never stopped wanting to prove the value of the writers I liked.

What then did we have in common and why did I last even two and a half years in the job? I think what struck and cheered me there from the first day was finding a group of people who assumed without a moment's doubt that the dominant culture of the day was not worth the candle, because the values it represented so obviously were rotten. They believed that literary affairs in this country were largely in the hands of an establishment which was frightened of feeling. In artistic matters, you must therefore, at whatever cost, trust your own experience and believe nothing you read in newspapers. I found this attitude wholly sympathetic, and nothing that has happened to me since has disabused me. Indeed the most heartening aspect of the London theatre in the last few years has been the growth of a constituent audience for new work who seem to come in deliberate defiance of critical taste. I believe it is partly the good work of the Court which has encouraged this audience, and its existence is increasingly reassuring.

The other thing the Court taught me was to value aesthetic excellence. At the time my sole interest was in the content of a play. I thought the political and social crisis in England in 1969 had grown so grave that I had no patience for the question of how well written a play was. I was only concerned with how urgent its subject matter was, how it related to the world outside. As I came to realize that no common beliefs held the Royal Court together, I also slowly appreciated that there was therefore only one reason why writers chose, as they did in great numbers, to give their work to the Court first, and that was the likelihood that it would be better *presented* than anywhere else. Here the text would be respected, the rehearsals would be serious, the commitment to the project in hand would be real, however bizarre the running of the theatre outside the rehearsal room. And by encouraging the writer with their great care for the values of presentation, the directors were actually enabling writers to say richer and more complex things than they would have been able to if, like me, they were bundling an exhausted travelling company out of a van and on to an open floor.

I believe that the Court in the early seventies was primarily an aesthetic theatre, not a political one. And the reason why it then lost the loyalty of so many writers in the following years was because it finally refused to move into the field of English politics, although it was presenting excellent political work about the Third World. A direct confrontation finally occurred between those who wanted the Court to be a socialist theatre and those who wanted it to be a humanist theatre and, no question, the humanists won. It is for that reason that many of the best plays of the seventies were not performed at the Court, because there was, in an older generation, a squeamishness about moving into a directly political field. I believe this was a tragedy for the Court, and it is taking time to recover.

1981

5

THE AWKWARD SQUAD
About Joint Stock

I've been involved in founding two theatre groups in my life. The first, Portable Theatre, ended for me in Marylebone Magistrates' Court some time, I believe, in 1973. I kept no diary in those days – I was young and events moved so slowly – so I have no way of remembering. I do know I shook and sweated a great deal, since I'd only learned on the morning of my appearance that Tony Bicât and I would have to appear in court. The charge was non-payment of actors' National Insurance stamps. Since we had relinquished the running of the company some time previously, we were both surprised to find ourselves still legally responsible for its present state – although, to be fair, I had recently seen its administrator at Schiphol Airport in Amsterdam drinking gin at seven-thirty in the morning, and might have guessed that the books were not in too solid a shape. The magistrate fined us – was it £35? I don't remember – and ordered us to pay all our debts. When the company later went bankrupt, we learned that your debt to the state is the one debt that can never be absolved.

Things have changed a great deal in theatre in the last fifteen years. In those easier days you needed less money to start a new company, and everyone accepted that theatres might naturally flower and die. The fringe had not been institutionalized to the point where companies fear to relinquish grants from the Arts Council long after their artistic life has been exhausted.

Max Stafford-Clark, David Aukin and I met among the ruins of Portable Theatre and decided that since we were all freelance members of the awkward squad, we were likely to need our own facility for putting on plays. All our experience had been with presentation of new work, usually of a modestly controversial kind, and we were all well aware of how producers' expectations then rarely fitted with either our personalities or our tastes. I went away, to be honest, with little intention of using that facility – struck much more by the way Max, unknowable then as now, was going through a phase of insisting that there was too much snobbery in the world about what people ate and drank. To prove his point, he created Joint Stock in conversation while drinking large schooners of viscous sweet sherry.

For a while we seemed to choose plays which we rehearsed and presented in the regular way, although our bent was for the pornographic. One of these shows, which was of exceptional quality because it was by Wallace Shawn, was later to be debated in the House of Lords, where its artistic merit was vigorously contested. But, unknown to me, Max had begun talking to Bill Gaskill about doing a period of work on Heathcote Williams' book *The Speakers*, with no specific intention of showing the result to the public. I was therefore surprised when I met Bill in the street one day and he remarked ironically on the fact that, as a member of the three-man Joint Stock board, I was now his employer. Only five years previously I had been the greenest recruit to his celebrated regime at the Royal Court.

When in 1974 Max and Bill finally decided to show their work to friends at the Floral Hall in Covent Garden – after it was a fruit market but before it became a roller disco – I was taken aback. The directors had re-created Hyde Park Corner by simply upturning a few boxes and asking the audience to wander freely from speaker to speaker. The evening appeared to be casual, and yet turned out to be highly structured. There was a great density of characterization. (In fact, I believe when the 'real' speakers came to see themselves impersonated, they were perfectly satisfied.) Since the play appeared on the surface to be plotless, there was none of the usual wrenching and shifting of gears to which a playwright's ears are especially attuned. There was nothing flashy or insincere. The evening was dry, in the best sense, like good wine. I had long known it to be Bill's aim as a director to achieve work in which the content of the play was in perfect relief – there was to be no impression of artifice – and yet sometimes in the past I had felt the very austerity of his approach to be mannered. Now, perhaps because his talents allied exquisitely with Max's gift for detail, the audience was actually presented with the illusion of meeting and getting to know the speakers at Hyde Park Corner. No more, no less. The speakers were in the round, unforced, *themselves*.

All three of us suspected that the main reason for the evening's success had been the absence of a writer. The directors had cut the pages from Heathcote Williams' book, which had provided the dialogue for the play, into slivers on the floor with a big pair of scissors. There was a general feeling, perhaps brought on by Max and Bill's recent directorships of writers' theatres, that writers always spoil things. Both the greatest English directors of the postwar theatre, Peter Brook and Joan Littlewood, had ended up without writers in their rehearsal rooms. Pauline Melville had lent Bill a copy of William Hinton's massive book *Fanshen* and the very impossibility of adapting it appealed to him. Yet he passed it onto me with a poorly disguised heavy heart.

A particular tension in Joint Stock has never been very

satisfactorily resolved. Writers have a reputation for being tied to one view of the world – their own – but in experimental work actors and directors must feel free. The actor wants to own his character. The director wants to control the evening. The company has been at its most successful either when using writers with very strong personalities – Caryl Churchill, say, or Barrie Keefe – or when working on shows in which the writer appears to stand out of the way of the raw material altogether. In *Yesterday's News* a group of actors sat facing the audience, using transcripts of interviews which they had secured themselves with British mercenaries who had been in Angola. The same technique served in *Falkland Sound*, half of which is made up from letters sent by David Tinker to his father from a ship in the expeditionary force, and half of which dramatizes, in their own words, the lives of people caught up in the Falklands War. Both plays, although apparently documentary, were more artful than they at first appeared. The company's touch was less sure when playwrights were compromised somewhere in the middle, not quite knowing whether to set down the actors' research, or to try and create a play of their own. With *Fanshen* Bill had little choice, for the book is nearly seven hundred pages long and playwrights, for all their faults, are good men with pickaxes.

Hinton is a Pennsylvania farmer who was in China for six years as a tractor technician. *Fanshen* records the life and struggles of the people in the village of Long Bow during the great land-reform programmes which Mao's revolution instituted in the late 1940s. I worked on trying to digest and master the extraordinary complexity of the book, while, in workshop, the actors flung themselves at whatever they fancied, more or less in whatever style they fancied. The writer represented reason, the actors imagination. There were certainly masks in the rehearsal room, and there was talk of puppet shows. Stylization was much discussed. At one point, I was asked to play a bird. It was important to the directors that the method of workshop reflect the subject and that it therefore be genuinely democratic. For that reason Bill once insisted as we returned from lunch to our basement rehearsal room in Pimlico that neither he, Max nor I should be the ones to suggest resuming work that afternoon. We would simply wait until an actor suggested it. I think we waited about an hour and a half.

After the workshop I went off by myself and spent four months mining a text out of the book. I threw away a great deal of the more obviously dramatic material, because I was not interested in portraying the scenes of violence and brutality which marked the landlords' regime and its overthrow. In shaping the play, I was very little influenced by any particular discovery in the workshop, but I was crucially affected by its spirit. Although Bill had thrashed about seeking to find a suitable style for the work, often lapsing into long and sullen silences, he never relaxed his basic intention: that we should do justice to the sufferings of the Chinese peasants. This was a matter of the utmost gravity to him. His criterion for examining any scene was to ask whether it was adequate to the experience the peasant had originally undergone. Although the subject matter of the play was political, the instincts of the company were in essence moral. We were not revolutionaries. I think that is why, especially in later seasons when it sought to apply the lessons of *Fanshen* to English material, Joint Stock became confused about whether it was a political group or not. In making *Fanshen*, none of us believed we could duplicate the over-turning we described. We knew any form of change here was bound to be different. But we all admired the revolution, and shared an obligation to describe it in a way of which its people would approve. The adoption of a rehearsal process based on the Chinese political method of 'Self-Report, Public Appraisal' might, in other hands and with other material, have degenerated into a gimmick. But here it had weight and was surprisingly quick and effective. The self-criticism was real.

At Christmas I finished, and a few days later was sitting beside my wife's hospital bed when Bill breezed in from two weeks with the aborigines in Australia. He took one look at our two-day-old son and said, 'Yes, very nice. Where's the play?' Soon after, he arranged a reading with the whole company. It was very long and lugubrious, and at the end people said almost nothing, though one actor shook his head at me and said 'Sorry'. Given the general gloom, I had no idea why I was not asked to re-write much more. Only the beginning was rearranged and that somewhat peremptorily. If I had been more experienced, of course, I would have recognized that moment at which a group of people, expecting everything, are delivered something.

The play opened in Sheffield in April 1975 to a refreshingly intelligent and multi-racial audience, then came to London. I was on a beach in Greece when word came that I was needed at once to work on a television version. Hinton had hitherto ignored the whole production assuming that, like the two previous dramatic versions, ours would disappear without trace. But when he read the reviews, he appeared in England almost at once. He consulted with his daughter, who had been a Red Guard, and then with officials from the Chinese Embassy, before insisting that the play must be altered if its life was to be prolonged. The BBC flew me back to his farm to argue with him, and I found him waiting with a list of one hundred and ten changes, most of which sought to rid the play of what he called – I am using shorthand here – my 'liberal' slant and to give it more of what I would call his

'Marxist' emphasis. A generous and decent man, he proved a wonderful host, even as we set out on two days of attritional argument, which resulted in my once or twice giving the play a slightly more optimistic tilt. A line about justice which I had hitherto believed to be the fulcrum was removed. The play still stood. If I ever felt resentful about this, I only had to remind myself that his notes had twice been seized, once by the US Customs and then again by the Senate. The writing of the book had taken him fifteen years. I had given barely six months.

The television version was, in my view at least, something of a fiasco. I had an early bet with Bill that I would give him a shilling for every time the BBC director said 'no' to anything which was suggested to him. After all the pain and profound argument we had had about how best to represent a revolution on stage, we were now in the hands of a man who believed that all you had to do to televise a play was to point a camera at it. Bill told me not to be ridiculous, but at the end I didn't have to pay him a penny.

Subsequently *Fanshen* was revived whenever Joint Stock was in trouble. It became our *Mousetrap*. Once, humiliatingly, I attempted to do a couple of days' directing one of its many revivals and found it to be a lot less easy than it seemed. Although I thought I understood the process whereby Max and Bill had done their work, in practice I was hopeless at imitating even their most casual effects. The spirit of the show was best guarded by actors like Paul Freeman and David Rintoul.

The two directors and I sought many times to work together again as a team. I asked Bill to direct a couple of my plays, but he both times turned me down. We all found it hard to imagine material which would suit us as well. In part this was because *Fanshen* describes a period of history in which people's lives were unarguably improved. When someone suggested we do a similar show about the Russian revolution I pointed out that it was quite hard, in view of what we all knew happened later, to bring the same relish to describing the heady days of 1918. It would have been dishonest. We tried to acquire the rights to Studs Terkel's *Working*. When it subsequently flopped as a musical on Broadway, Studs asked us to reconsider, but the moment had gone. I worked listlessly on Tolstoy's *Resurrection*, only to be told by Bill that I was getting nowhere. I headed instead to run my own workshop with Tony Bicât as my writer. I tried, for once, to work on less political material. But I lacked Bill and Max's flair for letting things run away of their own accord. Later, however, a friend was driving from Stratford to London with Trevor Nunn, who was about to do a workshop of *Nicholas Nickleby*. 'I have no idea what a workshop is,' Nunn was saying, 'I've never done one. Can you give me any idea what David does?'

Joint Stock, inspired by *Fanshen*, then chose to go co-operative, and all decisions were taken by group discussion. The actors were brought in to help run the company. Some fine work followed, and for two years they managed both to maintain a high standard of performance and to attract a large and dedicated audience. Usually the characterization had much more quirkiness and vitality than we had managed in *Fanshen*. Both Howard Brenton's *Epsom Downs* and Barrie Keefe's *A Mad World My Masters* had much more gaiety. And yet you sensed that the principles of the work were the same as those we had forged when trying to do a play about China. Although the subject matter changed, the ideology became a little stuck. I suppose I reluctantly concluded that an openly political way of working only pays off with dialectical material.

I stopped going to company meetings after a group discussion in which I called someone a cunt. Although I was referring to somebody who wasn't present, I was told by one of the group that she objected to my using a piece of her anatomy as a term of abuse. I replied fatuously that it had hardly been *her* anatomy in particular which I had in mind. Of course she was right, and I have never again used the word as an insult, although it remains the one English swear-word with genuine power to shock. Yet somehow the incident oppressed me disproportionately. An actor made a long speech about how the only purpose of theatre now must be to work for the overthrow of the Thatcher government, then left as soon as his best friend arrived to have a separate conversation in the garden. He had actually cried during the speech. The politics of gesture seemed to have replaced the politics of need. Now we were all to have silly arguments about words.

Of all art forms the theatre is the most susceptible to fashion. There is good and bad in this. There are times at which audiences seem to respond to an idea, almost irrespective of how well or badly it is expressed, as if it is already in the air, and nothing will now stop them getting to it. All of us sensed that was happening with *Fanshen*, and the actors and directors worked to some common imperative. Nobody was frightened. This is not the only kind of theatre I wish to work in, but the feeling has come upon me only twice, and the first time was with Joint Stock.

1986

6

NOW THINK THIS TIME
An Introduction to
the History Plays

I started writing *Knuckle* in the same way I had written my previous two plays – on my lap. Running Portable Theatre in the late 1960s and early 1970s was a full-time job, and I used to snatch what time I could to write, never admitting to myself that I was becoming a playwright, choosing instead always to see myself as a theatre director who occasionally wrote.

My early plays, people told me, were satire, though I myself had no sense of it. Looking back, I can see that their view was probably correct. Beyond knowing that my own schooldays provided some background to the farce, I have to this day little idea where *Slag* came from, and I have no urge to find out, either by reading the play again or by being forced to sit through it. I set off writing *Knuckle* in a customarily careless and lazy way, inspired by the idea of expressing my love of thrillers on the stage. But the sudden loss of my manuscript in a dustbin in Amsterdam concentrated my mind.

My early manner of writing had been to start at the beginning, fill a certain number of pages and stop when the job was done. I travelled with a typewriter. One night I made the mistake of leaving the first thirty pages of *Knuckle* in the auditorium of the Mickery Theatre, where I was then working. By the morning they had been gathered up and thrown out by the eager Dutch cleaning ladies. A search of the huge metal cylinders at the back of the theatre revealed that the garbage trucks had already called. It is one of the oddest features of those days that all the most doped-out children of the West chose as their favourite meeting-place one of Europe's most efficient bourgeois cities.

Having to start again did me a great deal of good. Since then, writing has never been so easy. It now takes me a year, or sometimes two, to write a play, but I am sure I benefited from Life telling me so clearly: Now Think This Time. I had conceived of a pastiche, and I suppose indeed a good deal of the dialogue of the final play still bears the marks of that decision. But indiscernibly, as I began to work again, a purpose emerged as well, to, subvert the form of the thriller to a serious end.

In this I was only doing what many had done before me. I have no snobbery about thrillers. From childhood they have been the form of literature I have understood best, and my enthusiasm is indiscriminate. I still enjoy Dick Francis as much as John Dickson Carr, whose locked-room mysteries, you may say, represent the pure detective story at its most refined. If I have a preference at all, it is for those who work against the form to make it do something to which it is apparently not suited. In Patricia Highsmith's books there is no obvious mystery except the mystery of why we are alive. She works against the expectation of the genre to make violent action seem neither colourful nor dramatic but commonplace, fitting all too easily into ordinary lives. She banishes sentimental notions of guilt.

My purposes were cruder and less well ordered. Although I have been generally accused of predicting capitalism's final days a shade prematurely, I intended Knuckle in fact as an exhibition of capitalism's strengths and some guide to its intense emotional appeal. Capitalism adapts; and in the early seventies was adapting faster than usual to a change of mood in England. Underlying *Knuckle* is the feeling that there will no longer be any need for public life to be decked out in morality. In the last days of the Empire, English capitalism still dressed in a bespoke philosophy of service and intended civilization. But now politicians were ready to stand on a platform of bad-tempered self-interest, with only the most formal claims on the electorate's higher feelings. Out for Number One was suddenly to be the acceptable political creed of the day. In this, *Knuckle*, God help us, foreshadows the arrival of Mrs Thatcher, who likes to be thought of as a revolutionary, but whose true line of succession is from her hated opponent Edward Heath. The press loves to call her a crusader, but the title is decorative only, mere camp. A crusade for yourself is no crusade at all.

This my unlikeable hero Curly Delafield discovers but chooses to ignore, thereby losing the love of Jenny Wilbur, who was played in the original production by the young Kate Nelligan, of whom Michael Codron had heard good things. She, Edward Fox, Michael Blakemore and I set off for our pre-London try-out with high expectations of success, although Edward, I think, had already begun to realize how inexperienced the writer was. Although the part of Curly is long, it has little variety. It is always going to be something of a chore to play a hero who, having made a discovery, chooses only to smother it. All too easily things can turn into a one-note samba. I learned a great deal about loyalty and courage from Edward for, much as the students of Oxford loved us, the West End public did not. The wind used to sweep through the empty stalls as Edward, disturbed only by the sound of the loudest bartenders in London clattering their crates, would step forward to buttonhole a small and indifferent house with yet another monologue on the moral basis of capitalism. In this he never flinched. I admired him beyond words. One evening, I am told, the Comedy Theatre was almost empty but for the near-solitary figure of Colin Chapman, the inventor of Lotus Cars. For some reason that I cannot explain, this scene has always inflamed my imagination.

Edward's ordeal had been prolonged by the intervention of Edward Sutro, a noted first-nighter, who had rung Michael Codron the day after we opened to tell him that he wanted to be remembered as the man who had lost all his money in the original production of *Knuckle*. After four months of this behaviour he had to be forcibly restrained from more trips to the bank and gently told that the rest of us had decided to call it a day. I was sorry to see that his obituary in *The Times* made no mention of his wish.

My other great debt was to the inspiration Ross Macdonald's books had given me. I sent him a copy of the play, and he wrote a kind letter back, under his real name of Kenneth Millar. Most of the letter was about the threat to the seabirds of Santa Barbara, but he also said he had read my play and that although he was flattered that I had been influenced by him, he thought the play 'at a tangent' to his own work. I cannot imagine a more diplomatic phrase to use to a young writer who admires you.

I am able now to be relaxed about *Knuckle*'s commercial failure. It was, I believe, the only serious play to originate in the West End that year. All the others transferred from the subsidized sector. But at the time the hurt of its failure winded me very badly. I was aware for the first time that there was to be something about my plays which would attract the most impassioned opposition. In the days of Portable Theatre, when booed offstage by whole audiences, we would cheer ourselves up by insisting that the violence of the reaction was a measure of the success with which we had hit our intended targets. I wish I thought this explanation valid, but it smacks of false comfort. Apart from *Licking Hitler*, all of my plays have hit rough water as soon as they left the dock. I have not been short of friends eager to tell me why this is. I am sure part of the reason is that I write in a way which is deliberately impure. Pure ideas and ideals are deflected and strained through imperfect personalities which distort them. People who like to think their motives are simple find this provoking.

Meanwhile I had begun to think about the war. I was born in 1947, and it makes me sad to think that mine may be the last generation to care about this extraordinary time in English history. Although I was thrilled by Angus Calder's proof in *The People's War* that it was the war itself which educated the working class towards the great Labour victory of 1945, I must also, if I am honest, admit that the urge to write about it came as much from a romantic feeling for the period, its secrecy and, above all, its sexuality.

After I finished *Plenty* and *Licking Hitler* I found something Alan Ross had written which catches this flavour as well as it can be caught: 'The sadness and sexuality and alcohol were what everyone was wanting, and war was suddenly real and warm, and this unbearable parting and coming together in the dark, confined spaces was worth all the suffering, boredom and fear.'

None of this feeling had I yet sensed when a fat man introduced himself to me, unprompted, from across the table where I was working in the Wiener Library. 'I am Sefton Delmer,' he said. 'I bet you have never heard of me. Yet I have sat as close to Adolf Hitler and to Winston Churchill as you are to me now.' It was a fine opening line, particularly from a thundering asthmatic, and it led me to read *Black Boomerang*, which is Delmer's own account of the work of the black propaganda units which he directed through most of the Second World War. This book provided the factual basis for *Licking Hitler*, and certain sections of the film do no more than recreate particular campaigns which Delmer originated, the most eccentric of which, although colourful, I omitted on the grounds that it was beyond me to make them convincing. Delmer himself, who is not represented, never saw the film, for he had a stroke a couple of months before it was shown. I had anyway chosen not to show him the script, since I took a less playful view of the unit's activities than he had done. To me they seemed to speak not just of England then but of England now.

Wise friends have told me that I should have left the metaphor alone, and that the last part of the film in which I bring the lives of the central characters up to date is the weakest. It is certainly the clumsiest in execution and, given the chance again, I would stomp through the years with less heavy boots. But I cannot concede that the intention was wrong. To me the story is not finished until you see that years later both Anna Seaton and Archie Maclean are trapped in myths about their own past from which they seem unwilling to escape. This theme serves me again in *Plenty*, but even in *Licking Hitler* it infuriated people, who asked how I could allow so fine a heroine to grow so convincingly through her wartime experience and yet be shown years later to have become effectively a victim of it. I have got used to the clamour for a simpler morality.

In the same way, feminists have been unkind to the film for its portrayal of a woman who chooses to go on meeting and making love to a man who has originally taken her by rape. They object that although such things do regrettably happen, it is the duty of responsible writers not to show them happening, and particularly via a medium which for the rest of the evening will be reinforcing the most abject sexual stereotypes. I cannot accept this argument, for to portray only what you would like to be true is the beginning of censorship. In addition, Anna, however flawed, *is* the conscience of the play. In *Knuckle* the issue of conscience is much clearer. Jenny sees bad things done and condemns them, but she herself is not much changed. Interestingly, in *Licking Hitler* and *Plenty* I found myself concerned with the cost of having a conscience. The clearest way I can describe *Plenty* is as a play about the cost of spending your whole adult life in dissent.

All three of these heroines were played by Kate Nelligan, whose Canadian background always seemed to suit the parts well. A strange misunderstanding once came about between us when I was directing her in a scene and explained that some short phrase or other was intended coldly. 'It's just manners,' I said. She could not understand what I was getting at, for to her manners meant no more than the art of being polite, whereas I, of course, being English, took manners to be a kind of formalized hostility, a way of being distant. 'Thank you very much,' we say, meaning 'That's enough of that.' This kind of code is second nature to me, but Kate had to learn it and observe it as a foreigner. She approached the part of Anna Seaton as anthropology, and her performance has strengths of observation which fit well with Bill Paterson's remarkable Archie Maclean.

Licking Hitler stirred up people's memories, and many wrote to me about their direct experience of a landscape I had only imagined. I have rarely been happier than in the days spent before shooting when I went to interview at first hand as many of the original black propaganda teams as I could find. Travelling such distances, it was hard not to feel that these people had literally been cast aside. I was in Cornwall one day, Edinburgh another, to meet men and women whose lives were publicly neglected and forgotten and whose original intense experience had long been lost. War brings together those who would not otherwise meet; that is its whole appeal. But then it sends them away.

We filmed in Compton Verney, a fine country house which had once served as a lunatic asylum. I had never looked down a camera until the first day of shooting. This was my own secret, which I only revealed later in the week. I think the crew actually enjoyed carrying a novice, teaching me as we went along. As far as I was concerned, the film was already shot in my head. The editing was only a formality. We simply strung together what we had, and there was the film, like a mosaic. I think we threw away barely thirty shots. This method of making films is fine when it works but of course highly dangerous because you have no safety net. If in the editing a sequence turns out to be misconceived, then you have no spare material to play around with, as I was to find out two years later, when I launched into *Dreams of Leaving* with a confidence which turned out to be misplaced.

Summer came as we worked; the make-up girls picnicked by the lake; and Bill Paterson, field-glasses round his neck, went bird-watching in his dressing gown, like Chaplin, alone in the Warwickshire woods.

I wrote *Plenty* alongside *Licking Hitler* and, because I directed them both as well, the different stages of their execution are lost to me. I know that some days I would spend the morning writing *Plenty* and the afternoon in the cutting-room with *Licking Hitler*. Made up of similar elements, they have, however, very different emphases, one concentrating on the war, the other on the peace. I had originally been attracted by a statistic, which I now cannot place, that 75 per cent of the women flown behind the lines for the Special Operations Executive were subsequently divorced after the war. The person who has had a good war and then can find no role in the peace is, of course, a character who has often been written before, perhaps best by Terence Rattigan, whose Freddy in *The Deep Blue Sea* is a brilliantly realized part. But I also had the wider aim of trying to set one character's life against the days of English plenty.

In England the opposition to *Plenty* forms around the feeling that from the start Susan Traherne contains the seeds of her own destruction, and that the texture of the society in which she happens to live is nearly irrelevant, for she is bent on objecting to it, whatever its qualities. This was certainly not what I intended, yet I can see that in the English theatre the counterbalance of the play, which is Brock's destruction, does go comparatively unremarked because it is the kind of death so many members of the audience have chosen, a death by compromise and absorption into institutional life. I intend to show the struggle of a heroine against a deceitful and emotionally stultified class, yet some sections of the English audience miss this, for they see what Susan is up against as life itself.

I became much more acutely aware of this when I revived the play in New York, four years after its original production at the National Theatre in 1978. The play proved to be a lot less controversial in America and enjoyed a breadth of approval which it had never known at home. In part this was no doubt because the American audience felt themselves much less implicated in the play's judgements. Although they found parallels with their own lives in the movement of the play – elaborate analogies were drawn with the American experience in Vietnam – they enjoyed the sense of seeing things at one remove. But they were, also, of course, not afraid to look English society in the eye, to see Suez as criminal and the Foreign Office as absurd. They also seemed less frightened of a strong woman.

Many people who had seen both productions congratulated me on my rewriting, especially of the second act. But I had done no rewriting except to change four lines whose references were too local. Why, then, did the play seem clearer? Why did the second act, which had previously seemed jerky and erratic, seem now to play through cleanly to its end? The only answer I have is time. Somehow time itself had solved the play's problems and put it in a perspective which helped it. Although we had meddled with the play's interpretation – Susan was a less isolated figure at the beginning than in the London production – most of our work had been done for us, by something over which we had no control. I cannot explain this phenomenon any further.

It's a common criticism about my work that I write about women whom I find admirable, but whom the audience dislikes. The truth is more complicated than that, but it is true that large sections of an English audience, particularly the men, are predisposed to find Susan Traherne unsympathetic, and it is also true that it is possible to play the part rather stridently, even forbiddingly, so that the audience watches and is not engaged. This was never my intention.

I planned a play in twelve scenes, in which there would be twelve dramatic actions. Each of these actions is intended to be ambiguous, and it is up to the audience to decide what they feel about each event. For example, in Scene Three, there will be some who feel that Susan does the kindest possible thing in sparing her lover's wife the knowledge of the circumstances of his death; but others may feel that the manner in which she disposes of the corpse is a little heartless. Again, in Scene Four you may feel that the way she gets rid of her boyfriend is stylish, and almost exemplary in its lack of hurtfulness; or you may feel it is crude and dishonest. This ambiguity is central to the idea of the play. The audience is asked to make its own mind up about each of the actions. In the act of judging the audience learns something about its own values.

It is therefore important that a balance of sympathy is maintained throughout the evening, and that the actress playing Susan puts the case for her as strongly as she can. The case against her makes itself, or is made by the other characters. This deliberate policy of pulling the audience one way and then another will work as long as the director has thought out exactly what the action is in each scene, and tried to present it as clearly as possible. For example, the action crystallizes in Scene Three at the moment when Susan hands over the card; in Scene Four when she lies bare-faced to Brock about letting Mr Medlicott down.

The time-scheme of the play is not as intimidating to audiences as it at first appears. Clues are built into each scene to tell you where you are, and how many years have passed. If the actors show the changes in their characters clearly enough, the audience will accept the passage of time quite easily. Brock and Alice both travel a great distance in the play. Alice is intended to be a historically accurate character, a bohemian of the late forties, part of whose charm must in retrospect seem to be her innocence. The path of dissent which she takes is very different from Susan's because it is mostly sexual. By the end of the play she is mellow, but stranded. Brock, on the other hand, has sold out, but, crucially, is intelligent enough to know that he has. It is always a mistake to play Brock as a fool. As a young man he has a delightful ingenuousness. Only an excessive enthusiasm can explain his speeches about the mortuary in Scene Three. But the institution of the Foreign Office takes him over, and life with Susan wears him down.

The transitions from scene to scene should be as quick as possible. If the director has to choose between amplifying the design or hastening it, he should always opt for speed. To those of you who perform the play abroad, I can only say that its Englishness is of the essence. To me, when an actor asks why he does something, it is a perfectly good answer to say 'Because you are English.' Irony is central to English humour, and as a people we are cruel to each other, but always quietly.

More and more I feel that writers have little idea of what they are writing. However much they exercise control by will, they remain for years ignorant of the true subject of their own work. Lately, attending a performance of *Teeth 'n' Smiles* which I had written in 1975, I was astonished by an incident in the plot which came directly from my own life and yet which at the time of writing had not then yet happened to me. From my point of view, the idea of putting these three plays together in one volume will be for me to have one more go at rooting out my confusions; from yours, I hope it will be to give pleasure.

1983

7
WHY PICK ON US?
An Introduction to
The Asian plays

The plays in this collection span eight years' writing, so it is important to make clear I am not a playwright who works to a plan. Each of these plays has a very different origin. Like most writers, I have very little idea why I am drawn to a particular time and place. I have more than a sneaking sympathy for the hostile Third Secretary who, when I rang the Burmese Embassy in London for details of the national dress for the character of M. Aung in *Plenty*, demanded 'Why pick on us?' It was not a question I was easily able to answer.

Nor am I an expert on Asia. If you write at all about that part of the world, you attract such gratitude from people who live there that your own ignorance seems more than usually shaming. Certainly I have travelled there, but temperamentally I am so opposed to the idea that research can of itself validate a work of imagination that I have moved about more to set me thinking, than with any idea that wisdom can be acquired by documentary means. There are, after all, package tours to the East these days. Anyone may go and describe what apparently is there. But a little travel teaches you that the Westerner, however peripherally, must always be present in your view of things. To claim to see the world through Asian eyes is, to me at least, transparently absurd.

Fanshen, in fact, is the only one of these three plays with no white man in it, for it dramatizes a book by an American whose understanding of China is profound. Yet my aims in writing the play were very different from William Hinton's in writing the book. Whereas he tried – brilliantly, in my view – by an extraordinary breadth of learning and mass of detail to give a portrait of how history bore down on a single village, I tried instead from the same material to write a classical play about revolution, setting out the problems which will always arise when *any* people try to change the relationship between leadership and led.

It is true that I conceive of the 'dialectic of history' in rather an idiosyncratic way. Like most people, when I have taken a particular course in life, then it immediately becomes apparent to me what the opposite course might have been. Perhaps if I write a play in a particular style, then its unwritten opposite – the path I never took – instantly becomes extremely attractive. I conceive of political process in the same way, as a series of compensations for strong actions. Yes, enact strong measures; yes, correct injustice; yes, change the balance in a particular direction; yes, give democratic power to the peasants themselves. But then develop a compensating mechanism to make sure both that democratic power does not become anarchy, and that those who have been robbed of power do not feel so alienated as to endanger your progress. History develops by a series of such accommodations. And the genius of Hinton's book is to lay out so clearly in what terms such initiatives and reactions occurred.

I have been proud, seeing a few of the play's revivals, to note that the play takes on different emphases according to where and when it is presented. Recently, of course, the question of whether justice is possible without plenty has taken on a special urgency, thanks both to the failure of idealistic regimes in the Third World, and to the pursuit of mindless productivity in the West. The play now glows at an entirely different angle from when it was originally presented in the mid-seventies. But certain things do not alter.

A European audience is asked to examine a process of change which is very different from anything they might anticipate in their own lives. For that reason, I try in the play to retain every situation with which they might identify. Unfailingly, the audience leans forward in scenes during which wealth is to be redistributed. Everyone wants to know what the criteria are, for they are all thinking about how they will fare when the moment comes. Once, in a phrase which I now think both pretentious and unfortunate, I called *Fanshen* a play for Europe. (It summons up memories of Katie Boyle and 'Luxembourg: *deux points*'.) But I hope readers will know what I meant.

I never used *Fanshen* as an excuse to go to China, for I felt that a quick visit would simply be frustrating. Also, to be honest, if I have written about something, I tend to lose interest in it. Orson Welles said that when he passed locations where he had filmed, the buildings stood like blackened teeth from which he had sucked all the goodness. For this reason, and a dozen others, I have never been back to Saigon, which now wears the thin disguise of Ho Chi Minh City. I had spent a very happy time there at the end of 1973, during the phoney peace which ran from the Paris agreement to the final collapse in 1975. During this period, the government was keen to encourage tourism. The beaches at Vung Tau, which were still in parts mined and ringed with barbed wire, were being advertised on unlikely posters as being among South-East Asia's finest. I did once bump into a single party of Japanese men with cameras, who, apart from me, seemed to be the only people taking advantage of the tourist programme. I was travelling around in buses trying to get as far into Vietnam as I could at exactly the time that so many Americans finally succeeded in managing to get out.

It took me a long time to find a way of writing about Vietnam, and when I did I was much influenced by a number of films which represented the war as an exclusively American tragedy. We were repeatedly told that Vietnam was a traumatic experience for Americans, but there seemed less regard – at least in fiction – for the Vietnamese themselves. I was determined that the balance of my story would be different. The senior bank teller Quoc gives the film its flavour, and the plight of the local employees at the end provides it, I hope, with its kick. I also tried to be true to my memory of one of the most beautiful cities in the world. It is hard to explain to people who never went there that even during the war life was extraordinarily pleasant for quite large numbers of people. By the time I got there, it was clear this life would soon come to an end, and yet by some act of mass suspension nobody ever referred to this fact. This, combined of course with the pleasures of the city, gave life a dreamy quality which was rather delicious, even when, as in the first part of the film, the kerosene dumps were exploding on the horizon. As soon as I realized that the American Ambassador had been, literally, unable to imagine a US defeat, I was able to begin writing. But it was not until I understood the behaviour of certain CIA agents, and appreciated that the CIA was regarded in certain parts of Washington as a dangerously liberal organization, that I knew how I would be able to present those final few months.

The making of *Saigon: Year of the Cat* was prolonged and difficult. Long before filming began, I was called in Sydney, Australia, and ordered to Bangkok where, I was told, the director was pretending to be ill. When I got there, a producer told me that Stephen Frears was a notoriously lazy and capricious man, and that the doctor had declared that he was simply 'tired'. It was to be my job to persuade him from his bed. As soon as I walked into his ice-cold room I knew at once that the doctor was a fool. I had Stephen moved to the English hospital, where pneumonia was quickly diagnosed. Far from being lazy, Stephen was insistent on working. He called a production conference in which he kept asking the art director about various sequences which did not appear to be in the script. The production team had only just met their director, and did not like to question him. They nodded enthusiastically when he called, as he did obsessively, for 'burning sampans'. It was only after we left the hospital room that I was able to explain to everyone that the director was delirious.

This was why I took a closer part than is usual for a writer in the preparation of the film. I also had to be present throughout its shooting, for we had employed a leading man who was reluctant to say any of the lines I had written. Mercifully, this is the only time I have experienced this problem. Frederic Forrest had worked with Marlon Brando on *Apocalypse Now*, and in his hotel room he played me a video of the long last scene ('The horror! The horror!'), constantly interjecting 'I wrote this', or, more often 'Marlon wrote this'. This film had convinced him that actors should write their own dialogue. It was more spontaneous. When I pointed out that this was much the worst scene in the film, he seemed not at all disturbed. My blood was chilled when he produced a school exercise book, on one side of which he had written out my entire text in painful longhand, and on the other, what he was actually proposing to say.

We began filming without having resolved the matter. This made life especially hard for Judi Dench whose method, you might say, is the very opposite to Freddy's. She will accept whatever rubbish you throw at her and turn it into gold. In *Saigon* she gives the loveliest of all her screen performances, silkenly sexy and intelligent as only she can be. Although Freddy's re-writings appeared at first to be arbitrary, it was Stephen who noticed there was a pattern to them. Not only did he want, in a rather Hollywood way, to make his character more likeable (though Hollywood-likeable, to me, is detestable), but he also was trying to steer the text away from showing just how badly the Americans had behaved in the final days. It was, in short, an irony. I was trapped in evidence of the problem I had set out to illustrate. My leading man did not truly believe that the Americans had lost a war.

I liked Frederic immensely. He is a man who is both honest and kind. I also admired his acting. But life was undeniably tricky. One weekend, exhausted, I took off for Chiang Mai without leaving a number and came back to find a scene had gone to twenty-four takes without one being accepted. When I finally left Bangkok, two weeks before the end of shooting, I walked into an apartment in New York where the phone was already ringing with the news that a strike of technicians at Thames Television in Teddington meant that our film would have to be abandoned incomplete. Nine months later we reassembled at Shepperton and did manage to finish. We used Battersea Park for downtown Saigon.

I was often told that our troubles were of my making. I had tried to stretch British television too far, by writing on a scale with which it could not be expected to cope. I think this is wrong. Stephen Frears taught me the great and difficult rule of film-making, which is never to accept anything with which you are not satisfied. By his fortitude and high standards he pulled this unwieldy project on to the screen. When it was shown, an NBC executive who admired it lamented to my agent that it would never be seen on an American network.

'Oh,' she replied, 'you mean because of the politics?' 'No,' he said, 'because a middle-aged woman is in bed with a younger man. That is totally unacceptable.' At such moments British television can be seen to have its strong points.

A Map of the World is a play which argues with itself, a play full of worry and confusion. Clumsy and disparate, it unreels in a strange and unpredictable fashion, switching styles, shifting arguments. For those who want a political play about the Third World, the long passages about fiction may seem frustrating. For the theatrically minded, the approach to character and plot development may seem perverse. Unarguably, I was trying to do too many things at once, and although I have now directed three productions of the play, I cannot ever quite achieve the right balance between the different strands. The best passages are still those which I wrote quickest.

I had been asked by Jim Sharman to contribute something to the 1982 Adelaide Festival, and implicit in his invitation was the hope that I might be moved to write about Australia. He even gave me a title – *The Dead Heart*. But my exploratory trip, although highly enjoyable, did not get me writing. On the way back my plane landed in Bombay, and my son and I decided to go into town for a few days. As soon as I walked into my hotel, I knew I had found a setting. The management of the Taj Mahal have since been kind enough to write and ask if the play might be staged in their lobby, but I have had to explain that its formal demands make this impossible. A similar invitation from Mrs Gandhi to perform the play at the Commonwealth Prime Ministers' Conference had to be regretfully declined.

I was obviously trying, as best I could, to articulate arguments which are of great importance to developing countries but at whose mention people in the West feel themselves, for some reason, entitled to glaze over. I found myself fascinated by a subject to which there was such in-built resistance and determined to make it live in the theatre. In this I was helped by all the work I had done with Hayden Griffin at the National Theatre and outside it, struggling with the problems of how to design epic plays. All too often the real pleasure of epic theatre – the easy movement of time and place – is lost in the gaps while the scenery is changed. In this way the flow is disrupted and the irony you intend by setting adjacent scenes in different styles gets spoilt as stage-hands in black clothing blunder about in the semi-dark. *A Map of the World* is a seamless epic. There are almost no blackouts. The changes themselves are written as part of the action. They have a rhythm which contributes to the meaning of the play.

Adelaide was a perfect place to open. The temperature was over 110 degrees, and the sky was bluer and wider than anywhere in the world. The air was bone-dry. We attracted exactly the response we had hoped for. In an ideal production of the play, you find yourself agreeing with whoever has last spoken. Performances were regularly interrupted by satisfying cries of 'Nonsense' and 'Right on'. M'Bengue, in particular, attracted considerable heat. A disputatious play, *A Map of the World* seeks to sharpen up people's minds, to ask them to remember why they believe what they do. To ask, in fact, whether they still do. Or should. This seems to me one of the things the theatre does well, and in return for those indignant or excited shouts, I am willing to endure a little mess.

1986

8

AH! MISCHIEF
On Public Broadcasting

For some years I didn't try to write for television. I had two main objections. First, I thought the studio process was harmful to good work and, second, I didn't like the censorship. I had started writing for the stage long after the Lord Chamberlain had been discredited, so it never occurred to me that a writer should be anything but free. I admire writers in South Africa, say, or in Russia or South America who have to accept the limitations of a dictatorship and who learn to work guilefully within them, but in a democracy I take the principle of free expression very seriously, even to the point where I doubt the wisdom of the race laws. So I am unlikely to take orders from bureaucrats about what I may or may not say in my plays, especially when as a viewer I am aware of how badly television has deteriorated in the last ten years. The row over *Yesterday's Men*, the banning of *Scum* and the cancellation of E. P. Thompson's Dimbleby lecture are only the most conspicuous of a series of incidents which encourage the feeling that the BBC is run by men who have made an unspoken accommodation with government: in return for securing the necessary annual increase in the licence fee, they have run down the service, and in particular its majority television channel, to the point of maximum inoffensiveness.

When Ian McEwan's play *Solid Geometry* was banned by

the BBC in 1979, just two days before it was due to go into the studio, the Head of Network Production Centre, Pebble Mill, made a graphic defence of his decision to me by saying, 'How do you think it would look if just as Margaret Thatcher was about to be elected, we were stupid enough to record a play which featured a twelve-inch penis in a fucking bottle?' (In fact, the script says *less* than twelve inches; but it had lengthened in the mind in the Head of Network Production Centre.) I admired his forthrightness, or rather I admired it until I received a memorandum the next day – I still have it – which reminded me that should this confession of motive be leaked to the press, I would be sacked. Well, time has gone by, I am no longer under contract, and worse and sillier decisions have since been made; but both the memorandum and the blatancy of the conversation confirmed what I had already sensed in the mishandling of the row about *Scum* – that BBC censorship in the late 1970s had passed into a particularly ugly phase.

In 1975, *Brassneck* had been the first of my stage plays to be adapted for television, for an earlier attempt to adapt *The Great Exhibition* had foundered when it was explained to me that references to exhibitionism were permitted in Light Entertainment but not in Drama. *Brassneck* was accepted; the script was in production and, so far as we could see, going well, when the Head of Drama suddenly threatened cuts. A meeting with him was quickly arranged in the Windmill pub on Clapham Common, and he offered to trade. 'I'll swap you two buggers for a shit' is the line I best remember. In fact, we'd cleared up the scatology in five minutes, and the wrangling only really started when we got to the 'God's' and 'Oh Christ's'. Even then, implicit in this public-house negotiation was the shared understanding that the whole damn business was too silly for words, that censorship was something degrading which we all had to put up with but which we all despised, but that for now we would drag through this meaningless game if for no other reason than to keep the Head of Drama in his job; which we did, and once the bartering was done, we drank more and honoured the agreement.

I cannot imagine such a session taking place any longer in the BBC. A new self-righteous tone has been adopted by men who often seem to take a chilling pleasure in the exercise of their own power. 'Nobody here likes halting a play,' they say, rolling the sentence round in their mouths, enjoying the taste. They appear actually to believe in something they call responsibility, which by the time it reaches our screens we may take to mean blandness, and in something else called editorial control, which I construe as them knowing better than you do, something which an artist (I know no other word to use) finds hard to accept in a journalist.

Differences in temperament between playwrights and journalists have been at the heart of many of the problems there have recently been in TV drama. The BBC is run almost exclusively by ex-journalists – sports men predominate and people from the arts rarely rise to the top – and there is a sense in which journalists neither understand nor accept the claims of fiction. They are bewildered and hurt by the idea that a playwright offers something which is necessarily partial, which is only an aspect of the truth, because for them, of course, the truth is verifiable. It is a piece of paper which passes across the news desk. They are most unsettled by the storyteller's central claim – that by compressing events and telling unrepresentative stories in personal ways he may reveal truths which are at least as important as the journalist's. The BBC's institutional panic in the face of *Scum*, during what was the most frightening and acrimonious of all its censorship rows, stemmed absurdly from the fact that its executives did not finally understand what a play was, and tried to apply to drama criteria which could only make sense, if at all, when applied to documentaries. Although they conceded that all the events in *Scum* were plausible, that everything in the script had indeed happened and could well happen again, their objections to its transmission were based on the idea that it was somehow wrong to cram all these incidents into one hour's television and thereby suggest they were typical of the whole English Borstal system. But, in fact, plays make no claims to be typical in that sense. The play *Macbeth* is not intended as an indictment of Scottish monarchy, nor does Shakespeare set out to prove that all Scottish kings tend towards murder. Yet an imaginary BBC of the seventeenth century, faced with that script, would have objected that Scottish kings *do not kill each other all that frequently*, and so the play must be banned. There is, they would say disingenuously, no 'balancing voice'. But where is the balancing voice in Dante? In Bunyan? In Dostoyevsky?

What is equally sad is how outdated the managerial tone of journalism has become. Because he has been brought up and worked all his life in authoritarian organizations, in the backwoods of Fleet Street, the ex-journalist cannot understand the violence of feeling his bans cause among the storytellers. Alisdair Milne's astonishing insensitivity to his staff during the *Scum* row sprang – I am guessing here – not from any defect of character, but from the fact that he had worked primarily among journalists who are well used to the idea that work can be spiked. Journalists have always been told that they must put up with having their work changed, for on a newspaper it is something which happens all the time. But in a theatre it never now happens, except by consent. Indeed, to an outsider, one of the main reasons for the general weakness of the British press appears to be the readiness of journalists to conspire in the massacre of their own work. They accept that their pieces will be cut and altered. They allow contradictory rubbish to be placed alongside their articles in flatulent editorial columns and, when asked why, will tell you it is because they cannot be bothered to get involved in the day-to-day running of their newspaper. Playwrights, by contrast, spend a good deal of their time defending and explaining their plays to management. They regard it as part of their job not just to see their work through to the point of presentation, but also to argue about the overall direction of theatres where their work goes on. They expect access to the boss, and they expect to be able to criticize the general policies of the theatre. Senior executives at the BBC are rumoured to hide from their own employees.

These problems in the drama department are now part of a wider unease at the BBC, which has come about through the growing rift between the programme-makers and the bureaucracy. In spite of the Annan Committee's harsh views on this subject, it is hard to see any improvement under the present regime. For whatever the statistics (is it one in seven employees at the BBC who is actually involved in programme making?), the major problem is to do not with numbers but morale. Programme-makers no longer feel that the bureaucracy sees its job as to serve them. Instead they feel that they themselves have been made the servants of a corporation which seems to be organized chiefly for the convenience of its own executive, and whose incidental product happens by chance to be television programmes. As a film-maker, when I receive any message from above, my immediate reaction is that I must be in trouble, for I can imagine no other reason why they are trying to contact me. If I hear one of the great panjandrums wants to talk to me, I assume automatically that his purpose will be to unveil a fresh scheme for butchering my work. I distrust these men, in short, because I do not believe they have my interests at heart. All around me there is evidence that, as in all over-inflated institutions, the chief loyalty of those in charge has come to be to the institution itself and not to its original purpose. The evidence exists that the executive has become deferential to government. They imagine that by placating politicians they will ensure the survival of public broadcasting. They are wrong. And if ever they were once right, the price has been too high to pay.

Television ceases to be of any democratic value if it cannot be trusted. The audience must believe it is watching something which has not been tampered with. The audience at present knows full well that a good part of what is reaching them is doctored pap. The pro-censorship lobby always like to claim that TV is a dangerously powerful medium, which an innocent audience often receives uncritically. In the early days this may well have been true, but now the audience, far from being supine, is cagey, highly critical and selective, and often caustic in its attitude to what is shown. Television, like the monarchy, now exists as much to be mocked as to be worshipped. Far from having too much authority, it seems now to have almost no authority at all. Many celebrities who imagined they enjoyed public adulation on television have found out how close the adulation is to contempt. Malcolm Muggeridge's elaborate disenchantment with the medium in fact seems nothing more than the performer's realization that the nation has perceived him as a vain fool. There is of course something intrinsically demeaning in striving too blatantly for national approval, but worse, the medium itself is now widely held suspect. The cries of writers whose work has been banned have only added to the public's suspicion of the BBC's integrity. The chronic failures of nerve, as over *Scum*, may dispassionately be put down to a misunderstanding of the nature of fiction, which by definition cannot aspire to the facile ideas of 'balance' so loved by the controllers, but to the public they inevitably appear as something more sinister – as the desperate bunglings of a frightened organization. The only way the BBC could now retrieve its earlier credibility would first of all be by asserting its independence from government (banning programmes the Home Office dislikes hardly seems the best way to go about this), and secondly by returning power in the organization from the carpeted sixth floor back where it rightly belongs: with the programme-makers.

For years, the needs and interests of those who create the work at the BBC have been subordinate to the determination of the executive to shape the organization into an industrial machine, and nowhere has this pressure been more disastrous than in the run-down of the film units and the insane over-investment in videotape studios. Years ago the decision was taken to build these stale over-lit shells in a great circle round the ground floor of TV Centre, and industrial logic now demands that they are used to the maximum and that all programmes, however dissimilar, be jammed into them. Whence *Sportsnight* is broadcast, there too must *Play for Today* be made. And yet this decision was made in defiance of the artistic preferences of nearly every drama director in the building. For although the public often claims it cannot tell the difference between taped plays and filmed plays, nevertheless when asked to name the single plays they have most enjoyed, nearly all will be films. Annually awards in drama go only to film-makers, simply because they have started with the incomparable advantages of working on location, setting up shot by shot, rehearsing as they go, and working for eight weeks at the end to edit their ideas into sequence.

My original feeling that standards were so low that it was not worth working in television at all were based on my early experience of videotape. The play is cast, rehearsed in a couple of weeks, then slung on through a three-day scramble in the studio which is so technically complicated and so artistically misconceived that excellence is rarely achieved except by accident. The eye is always on the clock. The pressure of time and the costs of over-running are so great that a director justifiably feels he has done well if he has got the play made at all. 'Good' directors in the studio are therefore, as far as the management are concerned, those who get their shows in on time. The process of manoeuvring camera and cast along this assault course requires such skill and patience that a rush of adrenalin hits every director at the end of his three days. Should he succeed in cramming the lot in, he leaves the box a giant, ablaze with excitement, crying 'We've done it.' Only an hour later in the bar when the rush is dying does he think 'Yes, but *what* have we done?' The truly hard questions can never be answered in the studio, because the part-hard questions are going to occupy nearly all your time. My own last memory of the recording of *Brassneck* was of leaving the box forty minutes after 'time' had been called, with an unrehearsed scene of a hundred extras and four unplotted cameras still going on chaotically downstairs, and the director crying helplessly to a random cameraman. 'Go in, Number Four, anything you can get.'

I apologized earlier for using the word 'artist' for it is a word which has knocked around with bad company and been discredited. Anyone who dares to call himself an artist risks the charge of arrogance, and yet his arrogance seems to me nothing compared with that of those who demand the artist's allegiance without giving him the facilities to do his best work. In the shambles of the market-place, there does seem to me an important role for the single voice, uncensored, the voice that promises to speak only when it has something to say, and which insists that when it speaks the conditions in which it is heard are under control. This should not be too much to ask. If the voice matters, if the voice is really wanted, then the organization will accommodate itself. And if this is in defiance of the ratings, if it is a voice less popular than David Coleman's, then the sacrifice will be made, and with good heart. Both of the directors of my early plays (one of them was Alan Clarke, in many ways the best director in television; the play, which was wiped and no longer exists, was *Man above Men*) were directors of the very first class, and yet they were forced to work under conditions which were simply not adequate to the production of good work. I determined never again to be a victim of the industrial process, and when I wrote *Licking Hitler*, I chose to direct it myself, partly of course to protect it against institutional pressures, but also because I alone was willing to wait a year until one of the coveted film slots came free at BBC Birmingham. In David Rose I found a producer whose allegiance to the film-maker is absolute, and whose distrust of the system, based on a far wider experience, was, if anything, greater than my own.

Film is free. Every artist worth anything in the twentieth century has longed to work in it because it is quick and supple. It has wit. Film passes effortlessly from style to style. By angling, by heightening, by the slightest visual distortion your view of your material may alter in the passage of a single shot. Film is fast. It cuts well. You create your work like a mosaic out of tiny pieces, each one minutely examined as it's prepared, and then slipped into the stream of images you are preparing in your head. I made my first film after eight years' work in the theatre, and I was exhilarated by the contrast between the two forms. The theatre is collaborative. There is no special virtue in the director and writer being one man, for it is in the nature of the event that it must be re-created every night by many people, each of whom must understand the exact reason for each artistic decision. If an actor is asked to move quicker in the theatre, he will at once ask why. He will need to have a good reason in his head in order to be able to justify his speed every night. And if the reason is not good, his performance will deteriorate. But on film, in inessentials, he will obey without asking, for he knows the basic truth of film-making, that only the director can see. Only the director knows how the images are to be composed; more important, only he knows how they are to fit together, and because every image must finally pass through this single brain, the actor accepts that his job is to serve, on trust.

Videotape lies in between theatre and film, the hopeless hybrid, recorded in slabs with unwieldy machinery, which, up till now, has lacked visual finesse, against sets which have no stylistic density or texture, and lit from a grid which is too high and too crude. I waited a year, and would have waited five, to avoid putting *Licking Hitler* through the studio, although it was often pointed out to me that it was set almost entirely indoors. 'Please go outside,' an exasperated controller said to me, 'just for a few shots,' as if that would somehow justify the use of film. But a sense of pace in film comes not from fast cars and busy streets, but from the movement of ideas. A film well cut indoors seems faster than a silly action thriller. Videotape, with inferior editing techniques, lumbers. Whatever the plans – and to the BBC's credit they exist – for trying to shoot studio plays in less rigid ways, whatever improvements you make by altering the grids, by changing the cameras, by extending the schedules, by shooting 'four-walls', in the last analysis the highest compliment you will ever be able to pay a studio play is *that it almost looked like film.* Not a true form in itself, it can only aspire to imitate another. Like needlework, studio is painstaking but dull.

One of the finest TV programmes I have seen in years was Robert Vas's posthumous documentary about the work of the National Film Archive. Ironically it was television itself which delivered this fabulous compilation of around one hundred and fifty clips from some of the films which are stored away in the vaults in Hertfordshire. For the first time, watching the extraordinary wealth of an art form which is only eighty years old, I began to understand the humanist claim that in its overpowering richness film approximates to life itself. Given the collapse of the feature-film industry and the shortcomings of the British distribution system, the BBC is now charged with protecting that tradition. Its job must be to guarantee the skills of the film industry in order that films may go on being made. I can imagine no more honourable or enjoyable task for a public broadcasting organization. Public television should be quite different in its priorities from the commercial sector. Even if it is forced to compete for audiences, its reasonings should be unalike. Ironically it is those who most believed in public broadcasting who were driven away in the late seventies by the threats management made to the freedom of the drama department's work, and it is those same directors and writers who long to return to the BBC.

At the best of times, television will always be a dangerous medium for a writer because he is so isolated from his audience. Any night in the theatre you may gauge moment by moment what the audience thinks of your work, you may watch them slip away in the space of a few minutes, you may *feel* their exasperation or contentment, but the television writer depends on the delayed response of a few selected people, mostly his peers, sometimes his neighbours, and usually his friends. He does not know at first hand where the audience has come towards him, and where they have drifted away, he has not had to endure their scrutiny, so he easily deceives himself. He is never put to the test of sharing his impression of the play with six hundred other people. The crazy statistics – eight million viewers for a single play – go to his head, and simultaneously he experiences a sense of unreality. Who are these eight million and what are they thinking? He easily comes to believe that everything on television is passing by in one nightmare stream of which his play is only a tiny part. When Dennis Potter argues that the audience cannot always distinguish between the plays and the dog-food commercials, what he is really doing is projecting his own isolation and bewilderment on to his audience. He assumes that because for him the experience of having a play on television is brutally casual – compared with the sustained experience of a stage play – so it must be for the audience. And newspapers flatter this view of television by appointing gag-men to be TV critics. The fashion is for writers – some of them brilliant, some of them not – whose underlying assumption is that here is one long spectacle passing by, which, it is supposed, will have variety but not density. The purpose of the stream will be for the critic to make jokes which will keep the stream in its place, where it belongs, in the corner of the room, a toy. So the playwright needs the steadiest of nerves, and a clear head to try and find out just what his audience's true response is. The letters I receive are compelling but eccentric. 'I saw your play and left my job,' said one correspondent. Another '. . . I saw your play and have left my husband.'

This strange botched-up medium is too good for a writer to resist, but too unreal for him to risk giving his entire loyalty to. Its very confusion is its appeal. Reith, for all his turgid moralism, was nearer to understanding what its priorities should be than the men who now seek to control its tone. Researching *Licking Hitler*, I found that one of the people who knew most about wartime broadcasting was the former Director-General Hugh Carleton-Greene, so nervously I went round to his flat to explain that I was planning a play about black propaganda in the Second World War. 'There can only', he said ominously, 'be one reason why a writer like you could possibly be interested in that subject; to make mischief.' At once he broke into the broadest smile, and rubbed his hands together. I have never seen a man so delighted by a single word. How attractive that spirit is in him, how fine the BBC was when he ran it, how much that sound working principle – 'ah! mischief' – is needed there today.

1982

9

THE DEAD HEART
A Production Log of
A Map of the World

Jan. 17 I arrive in Sydney nine days early for rehearsal, because the co-designer Eamon Darcy, who is working with my usual (English) designer, Hayden Griffin, has rung me to say he is having no luck getting the set through the workshop. The model was delivered three weeks previously, but no start appears to have been made. The first person I meet in the street is Nobby Clark, the English photographer, who has an exhibition in Hyde Park. He tells me there has already been an attack on my play – two months before it even appears – by some clown in Adelaide who says I can't write, and that when I do it's about drugs and hippies. I say to Nobby, 'How did your exhibition go?' 'Go home, Limey,' he replies.

At the production meeting it is quickly clear that the set has not proceeded because the authorization has not come from above. Christine, the production manager, is in that worst of professional positions – the executive who has no financial authority. The meeting of all production departments is therefore useful for clarification, but hopeless for decision-making. The tone of the meeting is not very pleasant – I am jet-lagged and the men in the workshop need much more information than they have been getting.

In the evening Richard Wherrett takes me to dinner at the Imperial Peking on the rocks, to settle old arguments, which we do amicably. It is hard for him. He is Artistic Director of the Sydney Theatre Company and in a sense I've been foisted on him. I was originally invited to write a play by Jim Sharman – who runs the Adelaide Festival (he also asked Sam Shepherd), but Jim doesn't have an actual company, so he's landed the Sydney Theatre Company with me. Because we have been rowing on the phone, this reconciliation is necessary in person, and plainly, on it depends my bloody set. The food is lousy and over-priced, but in the middle of the meal the *Oriana* leaves outside the window. My father was a merchant seaman and this was his boat. It's breath-taking.

Jan. 18 I always go through a phase of horror at the immediate prospect of having to start work. I get overcome with inertia and repulsion in equal parts. I am lying on a bed in a rented flat in Woolamaloo. It is decorated in various shades of green and brown. There is one paperback copy of *Lucky Jim*, my luggage, and that's it. Two weeks ago I was in hospital for an exploratory operation – they think I passed a kidney stone – and all I was thinking was, I hope this goes badly so I don't have to direct *A Map of the World*.

Jan. 19 I did look through the script, fairly listlessly. Because the play took so long to write, all I can see is the various layers, like rock strata. At the start it was called *Peggy Whitton*, named after the young American actress who is the catalyst for the action. My first idea was to dramatize a conflict of attitudes between two participants at a UNESCO conference. I can tell the exact point in the writing at which I fell in love with Victor Mehta, the fastidious Indian novelist, who is one of the two protagonists, and let him make his bid to take over the play. But I can also remember the moment – it was in Scotland, actually – when I became insanely excited at the idea of showing what happens years later, when an absurd attempt is made to film the novel Mehta has written about the conference. I remember thinking, oh great, now it won't be that most horrible of prospects, 'a play of ideas'. I can't stand evenings where people are reduced to their so-called points of view. I felt I'd hit on a great structure for showing the perspective time and personality give to 'pure' ideas. But now I honestly don't know if it works.

Jan. 20 A brief meeting with Richard settles the set – I make a couple of concessions, he also. Now it can go ahead. Melody Cooper joins to work on the costumes.

Jan. 21 The STC have fucked up the leading man's arrival date. Roshan Seth has been told the wrong rehearsal date. He has a job in Delhi which he cannot leave. Ann Churchill-Brown, who is Richard's assistant, is always now on the phone to India. It is usually impossible to get through. This work should have been done months ago.

Jan. 22 I am as much in the workshops as I can be, because good craftsmen are refreshing. Geoff the metal-worker and Ken the prop-maker are both brilliant. Penny Downie, who is my leading lady, arrives in Sydney, so we meet, I very nervous, she also, I guess, but more gracious. Richard has gone to a place called Dunk for two weeks' holiday. He apologizes for being away for the start of my rehearsal period. I say, don't worry, but that while he's away my philosophy will be spend, spend, spend. A joke which does not amuse him. Earlier he has suggested cutting a small piece of scenery. Why? I said, it's only three rows of *Chicago* (their current hit).

Jan. 23 Horrible weekend. Feeling terrible, wasting time. I go to see *Puberty Blues*. Am reminded of how Lew Grade said 'All my films are great. Some of them are terrible, but they're all great.' This, in the best way, is what I feel about Australian films, *all* of which I enjoy.

Jan. 25 Most of my day spent worrying about the back wall, which has to look like a film studio. Eamon and I cannot come up with a process to fake the felt-and-wiring they use for sound insulation, and the painter's samples are not good. From the first day I have said the work should be contracted out, but morale is so poor in the house workshop that this is a dicey proposition. They don't dare contract out.

Jan. 26 Melody's work is a joy. She touches me by believing the play is real. Of the end she asks 'Did your friend really die?' I can imagine no remark so flattering to a writer of fiction. *p.m.* I go to the cricket and gawp at Viv Richards, a few feet away. The whole occasion, under floodlights, is superbly managed, boozy and benign. The only dangerous moment comes when Nobby tries to take a picture of Greg Chappel returning to the pavilion after his seventh duck in a row. Chappel looks for a moment as if he'll hit Nobby.

Jan. 27 Another production meeting. The stage at Adelaide – a conventional picture-frame stage – is infinitely more satisfactory than the Drama Theatre in the Sydney Opera House. Everything about the Opera House is magnificent outside, unworkable within. But worst of the lot is the theatre we're in, a concrete letterbox. The set will look wonderful in Adelaide, but will have to be chopped about for Sydney. In addition, we will virtually have to put in a new flying system to operate it. At a later, more acrimonious meeting with Donald McDonald, the General Manager, I am arguing we need a couple of pieces for Adelaide which we will just have to cut for Sydney. They are refusing on grounds of expense. I don't see why the full intention of the design shouldn't be seen in Adelaide at least. At six-fifteen Ann finally gets through to Delhi, and gives Roshan the details of his flights the next day. The Australian operator tells Ann she has attempted this call eighty-three times.

Jan. 28 Rehearsals are due to start but cannot, so we delay a day. Sheila Scott-Wilkinson arrives from Los Angeles. I have cast her as Elaine without ever meeting her. The entire project depends on seven leading players, none of whom I have ever seen acting on a stage before. It is all hunch. *p.m.* Go to *Winter of Our Dreams* (Lew Grade q.v.). In the evening Roshan rings to say his flight was four hours late, so he has missed his connection in Bombay. I have written a play about chaos and India, so it is getting its revenge. I decide to start without him. The minutes of the production meeting are given to me, bearing little resemblance to the event I attended. There is a craze in this organization for putting things on record, another sign of insecurity. If you are trying to be kind, the minutes remind you of *Rashomon*; if unkind, of *Pravda*.

Jan. 29 We start. Hurrah! Nearly everyone is OK – there is one outstanding exception, with whom my future is grim. He will need hard work. I pretend I will be able to think of an end for the play, but I have no idea what it might be. As they have failed to get the leading man to rehearsals on time, I decide to demand my extra Adelaide scenery. And thereby I get it.

Jan. 31 Second day of rehearsal trailed out inconsequentially, because we cannot work without Roshan, who is still in Delhi. This casts a gloom over my whole weekend. It rains all Sunday, so I go to Doyles with my old friend Caroline Younger, and eat a very large lobster indeed. By evening a fresh message of Roshan's latest non-appearance comes and I am hopelessly depressed. All honest conversation about the grave shortcomings of the play with the actors has stimulated no solutions in my mind. An intelligent piece in the *Adelaide Advertiser* by a journalist who has read the play gives me the first clue as to how people will react. The long speeches, he says, are too polemical, and will of course be cut down in production. Over my dead body, I think.

Feb. 1 Roshan arrives, in excellent spirits, and reads very well. An excellent day's rehearsal follows.

Feb. 2 Eamon rang after rehearsal to say a new Assistant Production Manager has been appointed and is working on the show without my being asked. His appointment has destroyed what morale we have managed to build up in the workshop. Earlier in the day I was told that the two specially hired painters had not worked all day, as nobody had bought them any paint.

Feb. 4 A bad day, mostly from my own incompetence. The previous night Eamon was not at rehearsal so I asked why and he said, 'I was doing plans for Ian.' I said, 'Who's Ian?' and was told he's the Assistant Production Manager. He has been taken on and is now giving orders on the show. This makes the lunchtime production meeting rather tense, since the workshop are as angry as I am, and with good reason. Christine opposes some obvious time-saving decisions, for financial reasons, and I explode. Then feel ashamed afterwards. At rehearsal, Robert Grubb, who is playing Stephen, one of the leading roles, is very uneasy, obviously feeling that I bully him, that I don't realize how slow an actor he is. But I do – I just fail to communicate it. We run Scene Three, me feeling wretched. The blocking is foul.

Feb. 5 I work very hard so we can run the play through before Robert flies to Adelaide to be with his pregnant wife for the weekend. The baby is due on the first night. We run the first half and the play is clear – apart from one obscure passage which I can clear up at the beginning of the conference scene – but in the second half I lose concentration, partly because Christine leans into the room at half-time to say some furniture we were relying on could no longer be built. This extraordinary announcement – with no warning – leads to another terrible row upstairs, for I feel I am being blackmailed. Eamon has posted a fatuous memo Christine has sent him to the back of a flat in the workshop and this has not improved the temper of things. I should not let her interruption disturb my concentration, but it does – and the second half anyway seems to meander – I cannot find its rhythm.

Feb. 6 More production difficulties, for the first time of our making, not the STC's. Rory, the English lighting designer, arrives, does an elevation and concludes that the plans are miscalculated and the fly-pieces will be in view, through the whole show, unless some bars can be spotted – an expensive and time-consuming procedure. I have already decided to send Christine a letter of conciliation, but regret now having to do it when we are for the first time in the wrong. Also a shame because the rehearsal has been so good today. I try to put a re-write into Scene Three, which fails, but otherwise we sail along – Tim Robertson, Roshan Seth and Penny, who is the great discovery of the work so far. She had sent me, foolishly, to London a tape of *The Sullivans*, after I had cast her, and I equally foolishly had begun to watch an episode. It's always a mistake to look at anything an actor does once you've cast them, because it's what *you* see that's important. Her audition was dreadful, but I had taken a risk – and she turns out to be a fine and funny actress. The strange thing is she had not even been in the list of people the STC had suggested to me I audition, and she told me she had been amazed to get the audition for me at all, since she felt out of favour with the company. A lot of actors feel this way. The other day I picked up an audition list for the next show and was reminded of *Casablanca*: Claude Rains' line 'Round up the usual suspects.' Everyone on the list I had seen. Richard is not a bad or stupid man, but he has not tried to cope with the responsibilities of his near-monopoly. If you don't work as an actor for him or his friends at Nimrod, you don't work. In London, for better or worse, there are opposing orthodoxies, and actors may choose or be chosen by organizations which promote a particular style of work. There is a choice. But here there is no choice, and little thought has gone into deciding how that near-monopoly is not to become stale and cliquey.

Feb. 9 A great day's rehearsal, the kind you dream of, when everything gets better. The first act of the play seems vigorous and fresh, and Tim Robertson who has the small but crucial role of Martinson, the Swedish diplomat, suddenly slips into character, like a seal into a pool. The others are wonderful – Robert for the first time seeing the heroic strength of the character, not the satirical weakness, and Roshan goes on exploring. At the end of the day Eamon brings me a list of promises the Production Manager is trying to go back on. News from Adelaide, our flying plan is accepted and can go ahead.

Feb. 10 Scene Five – where the actors sit around – is hell to rehearse. Peter Whitford, who plays Angelis, is at the saddening stage of rehearsal when an actor realizes that the performance he had looked forward to giving does not actually suit the play. And he can find no fun or excitement in the idea of the character I want him to play. I can scarcely look into Peter's eyes, for fear of his disappointment, which I understand. As usual, the *moment* when you try to nudge an actor's direction is crucial: with Robert I moved too early and he resisted me. Peter does not resist, but his heart is not in it. We rehearse the rest of the scene, me with a mounting sense of panic that it does not make sense. At the end of the day, again, Eamon has a fresh list of things Christine is trying to cut from the production. I am so demoralized that I leave her a note, listing four changes in our previous agreements. But later at night I realize I cannot take the strain of her daily failures – and I ring Donald McDonald to make the whole thing an issue of confidence: that these must go through as planned, and Christine must be brought under control.

Feb. 11 Disastrous meeting a.m. Richard offers me no support at all when I most need it. He's like a punctured bee buzzing in defence of his family. I am at my worst, staring at the floor and exploding alternately. Nothing is resolved. The day's rehearsal is surprisingly good. In the evening to see a painted backcloth which really has not come off well.

Feb. 12 Horrible morning's rehearsal, me directing at my most fussy and external, giving the actors no space. I dread Scene Five, because it is technical comedy between seven characters. The smart thing to do would have been to concentrate on character and *tone* first, then lines – via improvisation – but instead I have forced the pace in the work, in a desperate need to see the outlines of my own play. This is the worst thing of being writer–director, that you want the actors to show you what you have written, at once. In the afternoon I am honest about this and we rehearse the end. Then sit for an hour and discuss the play's meaning, which is of immense help to me. In between I rehearse a short scene between Roshan and Penny, which is like clear running water, they are such good actors. At the end of the day the reality of my disastrous relationship with management obtrudes – loneliness and despair. I go secretly to audition a replacement for one of the actors, whom I have concluded I must sack.

Feb. 13 The worst thing about any kind of standoff is it makes you feel so stupid. Whether you're right or wrong, whether your case is good or bad, you always feel, hang on, a cleverer person wouldn't have got into this position in the first place. It's just dumb. Is there anything more shaming in the world than raising your voice and getting your way? It's double-dumb if you're a writer–director because you're torn two ways already. The director part of you has to be signalling reassurance and support to the actors. I know there are idiots who think conflict produces good work, but I'm not one of them. Actors blossom when they feel your trust in them and in the play. Which is where it gets difficult with the writer part of you, because all I can see are the flaws. For instance: I have worked out that a lot of people will react badly to Peggy Whitton. I know from bitter experience that if you show a character who is just like you or me – i.e. a bit weak, a bit silly, a bit shifty, a bit inconsistent – far from accepting this character as Everyman, the audience instinctively pushes him away with a great collective sigh of 'Well, thank God I'm not like that.' Peggy Whitton offers herself as a prize in a debate between two men. She does it out of a perfectly well-justified mixture of exasperation and bravado; she no sooner does it than regrets it; and a good part of the second act is given up to showing how she grows up unrecognizably from the character who made the offer. But the action is there, like a fault-line, deep in the play, and however brilliantly the actress plays Peggy, they will not forgive her. They will think she is stupid and American. They will think she is not like them. Just watch, they will push her away.

Feb. 14 Telephone reconciliation with Richard, with whom I am finally allowed to make my points about the production management, and he finally listens. But when it comes to the question of the sacking, he doesn't want to come with me and says 'Oh can't Ann do that?' So I go alone. Having been mumbling and inarticulate in rehearsal, the actor now suddenly becomes forceful, articulate and intelligent, arguing I should have put him on a probation period, warning him I *might* sack him – for he agrees his work has been poor – but I cannot agree. It seems to me humiliating to ask an actor to act for his life. But the fact I feel right does him little good. He is heartbroken. It is absolutely typical. You work with someone and they seem to be in a stumbling sleep. You move to do something about it, and suddenly you are trying to sack Socrates. I try to find the other actors to tell them. In the evening Penny and I go to see a well-known English actress in an appallingly slapdash and insulting one-woman show at the Regent. It is colonial bad manners – the English imagining they can get away with anything abroad. The only truthful moment comes with Nina's speech from *The Seagull* about the hell of acting badly. We leave at half-time.

Feb. 15 Breaking news of the replacement to the cast gives me a torrid time, especially with Tim who is a kind man and very upset. The waters soon cover over and we work. All the extras arrive in the afternoon, so I explain the set. The conference room is represented by row upon row of blue-green bucket chairs, which are visually brilliant, but hell to move. We work the changes. Exhausting in the heat, more like being a general than a director. At six-thirty the new actor Desiré Vincent arrives, and he and I work till eight, then my brain goes and we stop.

Feb. 16 Rotten day. First Sheila makes me feel like an incompetent, then Robert. They are both trained to think that by studying character they will make the journey to their parts; but they don't seem aware that what will actually communicate on the first night is their very own essence. That is what actors cannot help giving off – a smell of themselves. Grubb's job on the first night will be, in part, to be a happy Grubb. His job in rehearsal is therefore to keep happy – by freedom and experiment. Once you let panic into the rehearsal room, you are dead. But instead, Robert lets himself get hung up all the time on technical line problems, he goes into knots about things which just don't matter that much. I ought to be able to untie them for him by calm, and general approach. I can't. So I get knotted. The cast all like the play, but few of them think me much use as a director.

Feb. 17 Better day, thank God. I could not have stood another Tuesday. The worst thing is I know how to have a good day – by manipulating the schedule. To leave out the scenes I can't do. But progress and enthusiasm.

Feb. 18 A very good morning when I seem finally to get the spirit of the work across to Grubb inevitably ends with Grubb vomiting: first in the lavatory, then in Eamon's car as he drives him home. I can hardly complain this virus is contrived, but it seems too much to bear. In the afternoon we have a chair-stacking rehearsal, which goes surprisingly well. Equity meets to discuss compensation for the actor who is gone.

Feb. 19 Strange day. We dawdle until Robert returns. Then I run the film scene and Penny is excellent, but cries when she can't do a certain bit. I feel guilty.

Feb. 20 I start crying myself on the way in to work. I had forgotten what writing and directing a full-length stage-play is like; and abroad is worse. Robert is dreadful in Scene One and I have to speak to him sharply: he is not sulky as I had expected, but instantly improves – though not enough to make a run of Act One very enjoyable. The play is so competitive – each actor has to fight for his point of view, and in this run the black men win – Desiré and Roshan make the problems of the whites – Penny and Robert – seem silly and shallow.

Feb. 22 For the first time we have a proper-sized rehearsal room and the play breathes wonderfully for those who seize their chances: less wonderfully for the frightened, notably Robert, who invents a fresh excuse for not acting – that he can't work in front of so many people. (All the extras are in.) I have some sympathy for him – he has chronically misjudged his flight-path to this play. He thought I worked too hard and pushed too early – now he is realizing how far behind he is, and is panicking. If he is bad in the part, it is the play which will look bad – not him.

Feb. 23 The ultimate production department balls-up. Or at least let's hope so. An advance bar for lighting in Adelaide was asked for by us three months ago, and Rory has planned his whole rig on the assumption it has been agreed to. Last night we were told it would cost 6,000 dollars to put in. Everyone at the theatre agrees I am entitled to press for it, this time they are on my side as the Production Manager's failure is so blatant – but for some reason I give an imitation of being a nice guy and say, forget it. Quite why I have no idea. Though Rory agrees it is just possible to do without it. Downstairs, meanwhile, I worked hard with Peter and Robert Grubb, who finally claims a sore throat at five-thirty – his latest and last excuse for not acting – though to be fair again, he has made progress today. In the workshop this morning a casual worker came up to me and shook my hand, said, 'Are you the man that's trying to do it all himself?' I said 'What, you mean write and direct?' He said, 'You're very brave.' I said, 'What, you mean foolish?' He grinned and said, 'Yes, foolish.'

Feb. 24 Very nervous before the first run-through, but as it goes it strengthens and gathers power. At the end everyone is silent. There is nothing really to say. Once in a play's life you do it for yourselves and no one else, you don't really care why you did it, or what anyone will think of it. Penny and Roshan are sitting at the side of the rehearsal room wiping the tears out of their eyes. It is perhaps self-indulgent, but it is only once in a play's life that actors throw off their awareness of the obligation to perform, and the play really moves you. Today was the day. All else seems irrelevant. As that Penny is blocked on one side of the stage throughout Act One. Or that

Robert is not yet very good. We at least develop a bantering, adversary relationship which is better than the sullenness which has been our style to date. The rest of the work is now the dull and trivial business of whipping the play along – no doubt what's called 'improving' it. Yet its spirit will never be more touching than today. There is a state of disrepair when a play is not really for the public, when it is infinitely more 'real' than before it is slickened up. Now the slicking.

Feb. 25 Easy day. Perhaps a 'false sense of confidence. Everything we touch improves, effortlessly. A run always clears things out.

Feb. 26 The penalty of having eased up is of course that Robert's wife begins to claim contractions, and he tells me he has to go on to Adelaide tonight. This means we lose tomorrow's final run-through. The one we have is shaky, jumpy, unfocused, though the best of it is Penny's first act which is excellent, and the fact that much of Robert's progress has stuck. I have no impression of the play itself at the run, the whole thing is technical, needs work. I will be short of time.

Feb. 27 The day starts wonderfully with Hayden arriving on a plane from England with the music tape, which Nick Bicât has composed in London, and a Sony Walkman he has bought in Singapore, so that I can hear the music as soon as possible. It is excellent. We fly to Adelaide, as to a new world, for we are met on the tarmac by the wonderful Mary Vallentine, who is not only the administrator of the Festival, but more or less the best administrator I have ever met anywhere. For instance, not only does she meet you off the plane, not only does she say that she happens to have hired a spare car and would you, as a visitor, by any chance like the use of it, but also she presses actual dollar bills into your hand, saying she couldn't bear you not to have your expenses up front. She is sharp as a tack, funny, clever. All my best memories of my first trip to Australia a year ago involve her; crossing the lake to Gay Bilson's blissful restaurant at Berowra Water, or sitting all night on a balcony watching the rollers under the jet-black sky at Bondi. But when we all get to the theatre, the painting is disastrous. The work that needs to be done is horrifying. Profound depression.

Feb. 28 People are now working well on stage, thanks to Hayden establishing his authority, and Rory's calm. I cut Nick's music to timings.

Mar. 1 Foully heavy day which ends badly. Up at eight to check the sound – which is no good. New speakers needed. Then a run-through of the play in the world's noisiest rehearsal room at the Festival Centre. Then we begin a technical rehearsal, which starts well but loses concentration as we go. One actor is stoned, about which I am very angry, and by nine-thirty I turn round and have the unpleasant feeling that Rory and I are the only people whose concentration is still holding. Everyone else is completely flaked out in the stalls. Oddly it is at times like this you least need reassurance, but truthfully Christine is the only person to say anything kind: that the set looks beautiful. A strange reversal of her earlier position. I got to bed at 2a.m. senseless with exhaustion.

Mar. 2 Up at eight. An especially hard day begins with an idiot asking the world's stupidest question for an ABC interview: 'What's the play about?' I reply so truthfully that he turns the tape off, and tries to start again. Then the technical resumes. More hours in the dark – a truck which for six weeks I have said will not work on pin-bolts fails to work on pin-bolts – and then a dress rehearsal at which the acting is strident and forced. The first two scene changes are a complete mess, and at the end I lose my temper with Jim Sharman because he tries to refuse me a full show crew for the next day's work: I need it desperately, to clean up the changes. I

am annoyed because Jim has just watched the run and knows
how bad the changes are. But it's silly of me to lose my
temper. Brief notes session in the stalls. I ask Roshan to come
in next day at eleven and he groans. I instantly withdraw,
because this is the first ripple on the surface of what has up to
now been an ideal working relationship. Yet now, if I am
truthful, restoring him to the power of his performance in the
rehearsal room is my major task.

Mar. 3 Very satisfying day spent talking to individual actors
and cleaning up the scene changes is aborted by the cancellation of the dress rehearsal because Mrs Grubb goes into
labour – Robert does not return from the hospital. It seems
inconceivably bad luck. The cast disappear home in various
states of dismay and frustration.

Mar. 4 There is now an Emerson Grubb. We do a first
dress rehearsal at 11a.m. and it is fair hell, because of offstage
noise. The rostra are making the most appalling squeaks, and
there are far too many backstage moves. Onstage things are
erratic. I become extremely tense. We have worked very hard
and I judge we are due for a break. A long notes session. In
the evening the dress rehearsal is excellent – the one we have
needed and deserved. In the auditorium there is the usual
conspiracy of silence – nobody talks to me about this play at
all. As if they were frightened of it. Roshan is at his best.
Afterwards I buy him dinner – some ugly-looking veal.

Mar. 5 One of the oddest days of my life. A preview, after
which we are none the wiser. Nobody speaks to me at all,
except Richard Wherrett, who says it is superb. But this is not
my impression of how the audience sees it. The atmosphere
was electric, there were bushfires of response from all over –
cries of 'Right on' and 'She's right' at particular lines – but a
couple of gigglers in the circle alienated large sections of the
audience, and I felt no mass movement to the play towards

the end. Ideally everyone should cry in the dark. This did not happen. The evening was undischarged. For me, at least. There is a chronic weakness in the structure of the play – that Stephen has no scene with Peggy, to balance the one Mehta has. But then I realize Scene Three is in fact the love-scene, when they are left together with Elaine. But I never realized this until tonight.

Mar. 6 First night. We work quietly through the afternoon, me trying to get the cast to relax. I re-stage one scene further downstage, but otherwise just try and spread the notion of calm. I do this with such success that Robert begins the first scene with absolute lethargy and I become terrified. But the actors give a clear if low-key account of the play – much preferable to Friday's frenzy. The audience follows it all – what they can hear, for the audibility problems are chronic. Desiré, who is the most reliable actor in the cast, for the first time blows his big scene, but everyone else is good. In the interval I hear various comments – 'a political non-event', 'too contemporary', etc. – these are the remarks playwrights always do hear. Afterwards there is the conspiracy of silence among the professional attendants, broken occasionally by the much more enthusiastic responses of the public. In the evening all my cares flow out of me and I sleep.

Mar. 8 The reaction to the play is still not clear, and there are complaints about audibility. Tim Robertson's friends have declared the play 'vacant' – what the fuck this means I have no idea.

Mar. 9 A review in *The Australian* says the play is flabby and any other director would have cut it. Oh yes? Where? Peter Ward does not suggest. A wonderful morning at *Writer's Week*. I am overwhelmed at the warmth of the response. There are three hundred and fifty people in the tent, and we sell one hundred and seventy books in twenty-four hours. I am hugely touched by everyone's response and feel high as a kite all day. I go to the show in the evening and it is strong and clear, though I can already begin to see where it needs re-staging and re-writing. If Emerson Grubb were present, I believe he would be proud of his father's performance.

Mar. 10 A man called Radish in the *Age* declares the production 'creaky'. No doubt Radish knows best. A schools matinée for eight hundred children has them cheering the opposing sides in the debate. But the evening is, by all accounts, sticky and empty. I begin at last to see now for myself what the play is about. As if all the time we work in the dark. The play argues that as soon as something happens it is fictionalized. A past event is at once distorted, appropriated to support the private psychology of whoever experiences it. There is no perception without distortion. Nothing rests. Nothing just is. Everything is process. How to harness that process for good, how to use it and not just be its victim? That is what the play asks. This diary already passes into history, evidence of a private psychology, rather than a record of events. How to judge the 'truth' inside it? Would a life like Mehta's insisting on that 'truth' be a wasted one? Many years, I think, before this will come clear.

1984

10

A STINT AT NOTRE DAME
On Literary Fame

I recently came to America to lecture on one or two campuses. I am a moderately well-known English playwright, which is like being a moderately well-known angler or pigeon fancier. That's to say, to people who fancy pigeons my name is known but outside those circles, not at all. The fiction in America is, however, that writers are, by definition, famous. There is no such thing as a not-famous writer, or rather, if there were, nobody would want to meet them, so we all conspire in this fantasy that I am well known. The moment I arrive at South Bend airport to lecture at the Sophomore Literary Festival at Notre Dame, I pass into the fantasy, and it is important that I, most of all, should not be the person who spoils it.

Notre Dame is a Catholic university, and for a week before I speak they have been presenting a play of mine called *Teeth 'n' Smiles* in the students' own production, but shorn of any material that might be offensive to their religion, or rather to the stewards of their religion. As the play is about sex, drugs and rock 'n' roll, very little of it is left by the time it reaches the university stage, and it proceeds in a surreal series of fits and starts. Snatches of dialogue bearing no apparent relation to each other flare up and are suddenly extinguished. Characters jump into life, then fizzle out, as if silently removed with the hand of God over their mouths, usually just as they are about to swear, shoot up, or burst into song. Certain scenes, as when a medical student lets a dismembered finger he has smuggled out of the mortuary drop through his flies to the ground, are not attempted at all. It is a curious version of my work, and yet although it makes no narrative sense at all, the mere fact of it being presented in any form is enough for its audience, who cheer, clap, throw beer cans and generally make it plain they have found a rallying point. I am grateful – no writer is going to turn away praise – but also confused.

I have not yet prepared my lecture because first I am going to see what other people say, what the form is. First to go ('keynote speaker') will be John Barth, who does a lot of these things; in fact he does one a month. I calculate from the amazing amount of money they are paying me I could certainly live on one of these a month for the rest of my life: an altogether easier living, in fact, than writing plays. At dinner, before he speaks, Barth says that people commonly tell him that it's impossible to imagine Virginia Woolf or Marcel Proust wanting to read their work on campus. He always replies, 'No, but Mark Twain or Charlie Dickens would have leapt at the chance.'

When Barth walks out that night there are seven hundred students packed into a room that holds four hundred. This, it's explained to me, is in part because he's 'taught'. Living writers divide into two categories: the 'taught' and the 'untaught'. (Somehow I am 'half-taught'.) Barth reads a story about the struggle of a spermatozoon to reach a distant ovum. He reads it at full dramatic pitch, like a barnstorming nineteenth-century actor, and it is received with a rapture which would seem immoderate were a cripple to win an Academy Award. He goes on to explain that PBS have commissioned six leading American novelists to write single plays for Channel 13 on a theme of their choice, and that he has decided to dramatize the ovary's reply to the approaching sperm. No doubt David Hare will be horrified, he says.

After the talk we are all going to a party – there is a party every night before each lecture and another after – and there is some problem about who is to go in which car. The boy who is to take me pauses while we are still in the parking lot with his hand on the gear-stick and says, 'I want to tell you, Mr Hare, it is a great privilege to be giving you a lift.' English, I mumble something self-deprecating, which he covers at once. 'No, no, let's be serious. You are the most important person ever to have been in this car.' I admit this thought keeps me going for a while.

Back at the motel next morning I draft what I shall say – everyone has asked me to speak on what I feel about the censorship of my play – and in the afternoon I listen to the Israeli short-story writer John Auerbach explain his theory that what he calls the Age of Civility is now over. Citing the behaviour of the PLO, he argues that in the last five years mankind has definitively passed into a new black age, which he calls the Age of Barbarism. The arrival of this new Age of Barbarism is received with impeccable politeness by the students of Notre Dame, who applaud and ask the questions that arise from his theme – 'Do you think mankind has a future?' and so on. Auerbach answers pleasantly, with the utmost charm.

When I walk out later there are fewer people there than for the 'taught', but they seem warm.' 'May I say how pleasant it is to be here and to be so warmly received, especially by a militant religious sect like your own?' Well, there is no holding them back on this. A few people rise to their feet and cheer, others cannot actually manage this because they are beating their heads against the pillars of the hall, so uncontrollable is their laughter, and when later I say about the censorship of my play that I object to it on the simple grounds that I have never been aware of a Catholic playwright being asked to cut *his* work on the grounds that all those references to God might offend *me*, a humanist, there is such joy in the hall that I feel at first embarrassment, and then, I admit it, shame.

My talk is the usual writer's mish-mash, but its spine is a theory I have, conveniently, that America's gift is for the aesthetic, not for the moral arts. I am arguing that it is no coincidence that America has the greatest ballet and modern architecture in the world, that as a nation it cares desperately about how things look and feel and sound, but that when it comes to those arts which are most concerned with the question of how people behave, or possibly how they ought to behave, America is not exactly a world-beater, certainly not in the theatre or in television. This argument will lead me to the conclusion that 'the restaurant is now the great native American art form', but I realize long before I get to this pronouncement that there is no chance of my getting it out without pandemonium breaking out, and, throw it away as best I can, it duly makes its mark. Beer cans explode, the backs of the seats take a beating, there are those strange tribal 'whoops' of the kind which greet Johnny Carson when he comes out from behind the curtain. I have begun to stutter, to mumble, to mutter, to cut all my best jokes, to do everything I can *not* to pander to my audience, to tone down every smart-arse statement masquerading as insight, and yet ... and yet there is something inexorable in the occasion which will defeat even the most diffident or stubborn or incompetent speaker: this is a campus cabaret and it has its own impetus.

Next day at my workshop (a sort of post-coital gathering at which last night's performance is discussed) I try to be as dull as I can. I get washed helplessly into the general tone. Do I believe in progress? Yes. But does the quality of life improve just because life expectancy does? Well, I say, I start from the general principle that it is better to be alive than dead . . . And so on, more of this kind of thing. As I speak, I notice sitting on a chair at the front a young woman, very calm, who seems unlike the other students. And sure enough, when the talk is over, the rush of energy is to her, because she is Jayne Ann Phillips, the author of *Black Tickets*, and tonight's speaker. The magic baton has passed to her.

At that airport I read in the Festival Programme that her gift 'is for drawing the reader into the silent sobbing of human interaction'. Meanwhile I am trying to get re-routed via Chicago, because my Detroit connection is full, and the girl behind the desk is taking no notice. She does not realize how much pleasure I am getting from not being listened to again. How strange this need America has of 'the writer', greater perhaps than its need to read what he writes. In case I feel flattered, the student newspaper headline puts the occasion in its place: 'Hare humours moderate-sized audience'. Just so.

1980

11

WRITERS AND THE CINEMA
On *Wetherby*

One thing nobody seems to notice about the British film industry is how happy so many writers are looking. The history of the movies is always presented as a dire warning to anyone who wants to be a screenwriter. A Paramount executive summed up early Hollywood attitudes by remarking, 'We like to keep fresh blood filtering through the writing department.' But what is most remarkable about British films of recent years is how many of them reach the screen in something like the shape their authors intended. American screen credits tend to read like the name of some outrageously expensive firm of lawyers. Here the screen is illuminated with the simple legend: 'Robert Bolt'.

Television is blamed for everything in this country, especially by cineastes who think that too few feature film directors have a sense of style, because they have learnt the lousy habits of realism in television. There may be some truth in this, though the work of Terry Gilliam, say, or Stephen Frears hardly suggests that a training on the small screen has restrained their ambition. But television has certainly brought benefits as well. It teaches respect for the text. In the BBC of the late seventies, a writer was far more likely to have his script travestied by bureaucratic censorship than by any high-handed director. The real threat was from Milne and

Trethowan, whose blue pencils quivered over TV in a state of permanent excitation.

Now, largely thanks to Channel 4, a small window has opened and writers are pouring through, some falling over each other as they come, because there is briefly to be a chance of working in a million-pound form which is also, by some freak of history, *free*. Two years ago I started work on *Wetherby*. At the time *Plenty* was running on Broadway, and I was faced with the choice of either rehearsing a new cast into the production, or of throwing away my success – the ultimate madness, in American eyes – by going away to develop the strange idea I had about a middle-aged woman in the English provinces whose life is blown apart by a sudden, arbitrary act of violence. I was accused by the management of a suicidal wilfulness, and of course of 'betraying' the stage. It was hard to explain that an idea must find its own shape. The aim I had of contrasting the ordinariness of people's lives with the operatic passion of their unspoken feelings could only be achieved through the freedom and subtlety of film. In any narrative in which dream plays a large part, film wins hands down.

I set off on my course, knowing all the horror stories, yet fundamentally believing that the eye which first sees the dream should also recreate it. Our money was painfully acquired, in the face of considerable opposition, but with the help of Simon Relph and Patsy Pollock, stubborn characters who believe that to do the awkward film is much more fun. Unlike in the theatre, once the money is in your hands, you are free to spend it in any way you choose. This seems to me the most exciting challenge of film: that you may decide your own priorities. You may, if you like, spend your million to secure a week's work from Robert Redford. Or you can spend it on ten years' time-lapse photography. I managed to acquire

Vanessa Redgrave, Judi Dench and Ian Holm, which I always knew was a considerable bargain, and still have money left over to try and create the feeling of a small Yorkshire town with the help of a scaffolding structure which we built in a field outside Rickmansworth. I apologize in advance to the real Wetherby, but their town, which we all know from so many signposts on the A1, would have been too expensive. Besides this is a Wetherby of my imagination.

There is no special value, of course, in films being true to their writers if the work is not thereby distinctive; some might say, distinctively better than the films which are achieved through all the old studio arguments and confrontations.

Well, perhaps. But I refuse to believe there is not something especially satisfying in the work of Neil Jordan and Bill Forsyth, two outstanding new film-makers, both writers who now see their work all the way through and into the cinema. How long this present period of comparative tolerance will last nobody knows. The government is already threatening us with its short-sighted Films Bill. It seems set on destroying any sector of the economy where excellence has been achieved by enlightened subsidy. Britain is hardly known for its politicians, but for its plays and films. To set about destroying them is the politics of envy, indeed.

1985

12

SAILING DOWNWIND
On *Pravda*

It is bewildering, as well as enjoyable, for a playwright to walk into the Monday matinée of a play he has helped open some eighteen months previously and find the audience on its feet and cheering. It is not exactly something I am used to.

Recently the box office at the National Theatre had to take on four extra staff to cope with the demand occasioned by the announcement that *Pravda* will finally close on 20 November. I keep remembering Larkin's phrase about 'success so huge and wholly farcical'. Not for a moment do I think this phenomenon is of my making. Like *The Little Hut* or *Chu Chin Chow*, *Pravda* is a play which, for some reason, hit its own time. Possibly *Pravda* will vanish as completely and suddenly as the previous two.

At the beginning of the first preview, before the audience had been given a single line which they could remotely acknowledge to be witty, there was a happy shudder of laughter, as if the very prospect of the play was already doing its work. Howard Brenton and I looked at each other amazed that, for once, we were about to offer the public a play which they knew they wanted, even before it had started. We were sailing downwind. No, more than that; we were being *willed* downwind, by a great gust of public sentiment.

It is believed that Howard and I regularly update *Pravda*.

There has been no need. During its long run, different parts of the evening have glowed, as various pieces of wild satire have transformed themselves effortlessly into prophecy. When Rupert Murdoch acquired American citizenship in order to buy some television stations, he was only imitating our central character Lambert le Roux's earlier and more prescient assumption of British citizenship. (Later, Murdoch was revealed to be printing the *New York Post* on South African newsprint.)

During the Westland affair, our second act came regularly to a halt as our characters spoke lines, written a year previously, about the difference between 'leaks' and 'government briefings'. Chernobyl heightened the excitement, briefly, during our plutonium scenes. And when England's cricket team returned from the West Indies, the brain-damaged captain in our play struck a note which the audience seemed to find disturbingly topical.

Because of the eerie coincidence of life and art, most of the attacks in the press on *Pravda* have not been on the play itself, but on its success. Critics are not shocked by the characters – the craven journalists, the duplicitous editors, the insane proprietors – but by the fact that our portrayal of these characters was at once greeted and acclaimed as the truth by such a large proportion of the audience. For a while, I am told, reporters at the *Daily Mail* called across the newsroom to one another in exclusively South African accents. For others, it must have been a disconcerting experience to come and sit in an auditorium where they were forced to breathe in the heady air of revenge. A readership was expressing (loudly) their view of the papers they read, and of their fawning relationship to the government.

Paul Johnson was, I believe, the first to weigh in, wrongly taking the play to be an assault on newspaper owners. (Is it superfluous to add that at the time he had not actually *seen* the play?) In fact, we are much harder on journalists themselves, whose lack of both spine and mutual solidarity contrasts with the behaviour of workers in happier and healthier professions. An Edwardian cricket team of commentators then strode out to the wicket. M. Hastings had a go. Then A. Watkins. E. Pearce followed. And then W. Rees-Mogg. Last to bat was B. Levin, whose piece I heard of four days after it appeared. I rang the theatre and asked them to read it out to me. The unlucky secretary given the job had to keep stopping and going back, until, in despair, she said, 'I'm sorry, this is so badly written I can't make head or tail of it.' Levin's very anger had reduced him to incoherence, across four columns on the Op-Ed page of *The Times*. The man of many words, in the face of hostility, was lost for any which made sense.

It has since been claimed that the Murdoch Press's subsequent aimless vilification of Peter Hall was prompted by rage about *Pravda*. I do not for one moment believe this. In Britain, a great deal of what appears in newspapers about the theatre and television is motivated by simple jealousy. By and large American tourists do not pile off planes at Heathrow, asking how soon they can buy a hot edition of the latest *Sunday Times*. They ask the way to *Cats* and the National Theatre. Journalists know this, and it annoys them. The irony of the past two years is that Howard and I are now taken to be some sort of pundits on Fleet Street, a status to which we do not in the slightest aspire. From all over the world, I am sent cuttings from people who expect me to be interested in movements and excesses of various mad press barons. I am solicited by television companies for my views on various newspapers, most recently *The Independent*, about which I can say very little except that it looks suspiciously like the paper Andrew May dreams up in *Pravda* 'which will be decent and honest'.

What, then, am I left with apart from an unqualified admiration for Tony Hopkins and Bill Nighy, and a sense of gratitude to the three different casts who surrounded them? Simply this: theatrical success is evanescent. We wrote the play not because we were specially interested in Fleet Street. To us, it was only a background. We wanted to rewrite *Richard III* and ask again the old question about why and how evil is so attractive. If the play is remembered a day after it closes, it will be because of this. We'll see.

1986

13

AN UNACCEPTABLE FORM
On *The Knife*

In the early spring days of 1981 the English composer Nick Bicât approached me with the idea of writing an opera about the price a man must pay if he chooses to become a woman. It was a couple of years before we found the right lyricist, but when Tim Rose Price was recommended to us the whole venture took off, and by the time I started a company at the National Theatre in 1984 we had thirty minutes of material to play to the Artistic Director Peter Hall and to my old friend and colleague Richard Eyre. It was apparent to us all that we would be needing performers whose acting and singing were seamless. Everyone present expressed doubts about whether we would find such people in England, where the tradition of musical theatre is not rich. So we resolved to go to America, as so many immigrants had before us, to achieve something which we believed to be impossible at home.

The story of *The Knife* centres on a hotel chef called Peter, an apparently ordinary father of three, who leaves his wife and children, and, befriended by a girl called Jenny who has been damaged in her relationships with men, sets off for North Africa to change sex. From the very beginning we conceived the rather startling idea that the same actor should play a man in the first act, and the woman (Liz) whom he subsequently becomes, in the second. We took the project to Joe Papp, the director of the New York Shakespeare Festival, because we wanted a producer who had some experience of first-rate musicals. The man who produced *A Chorus Line* seemed ideal. He financed a workshop in the summer of 1986. During an exhausting two weeks we wrote a further forty minutes of music and words. We presented the result to an audience of eighty people, one afternoon in June. As soon as we finished, Joe came to us, his eyes full of tears, and asked us to finish the show as soon as we could. In January we started three weeks' rehearsal, then presented twenty-seven previews in the Newman Theatre before opening to vitriolic reviews in all major publications (*The New York Times*, *The New York Post*, *The New York Daily News*, *New York*, *The New Yorker*). The show then played to full-ish houses for its allotted run. It was almost invariably cheered at its conclusion. At the last performance a lady in her seventies said, loud enough to be heard throughout the auditorium, 'Well, fuck Frank Rich.' Her companions, shocked by her language, looked at her. 'Well, if they can sing it on stage, I can say it out here.' We closed on schedule on 5 April.

These, then, are the facts about *The Knife*, which are not in contention, as best I may set them down. *The Knife* was, for all sorts of reasons, not least the closeness of the team who created it, one of the more remarkable experiences of my theatrical life. Once we opened we were buoyed up by a very mild, but detectable groundswell of what could pretentiously be called popular opinion. It was enough anyway to ensure that my mailbag bulged in a way that only happens when people have been outraged by what they have read. Audiences began to arrive at the box office with newspapers in their hands, bearing the offending reviews, as if in deliberate defiance of what they had been told to think. We had all been warned that the *New York Times* was the sole arbiter of a show's life or death, so we were proud to demonstrate that, while we skulked downtown at least, this was not true. There was, however, nowhere to report on this discovery. You might think that *The Times* would be relieved to hear that it did not carry the huge burden of responsibility generally attributed to it. But no. When I rang offering them a short piece, they went back on a previous promise and explained they could only carry feature articles about plays or films which were provenly successful. People, they said, were only interested in success. When I conveyed to them that my whole point would be to show the way in which *The Knife* was becoming a sort of success, they quickly re-defined success, as being not what *is* success, but what *The Times* deems to be success. Would I be interested to write a piece for them to celebrate the twenty-fifth anniversary of the first James Bond film? I said I was not altogether sure I was the right man.

Joe Papp had contributed more and more to *The Knife* as the weeks of rehearsal had gone by. He was, as far as I was concerned, a model producer, diligent, helpful, intelligent, endlessly probing the show's faults, questioning its storyline, drawing my attention to little bits of the production that were falling out of shape. So it was natural that as authors of the show, we found ourselves in Joe's office in the long, hurtful afternoons after the show had opened, trying to work out what on earth had happened. All four of us were in a mood of profound discontent. We had a sort of *samizdat* reputation. People were coming. Yet we had no chance either of moving the musical to Broadway where it might attract the mass audience we wanted, or of generating the huge volume of hype which attended *Les Misérables* and *Starlight Express*, both of which had opened in the same week as us. We were a little skiff, about to be crushed between these two great ocean tankers.

We were all in a mood of genuine and rather painful soul-searching. We were keen not to blame our imminent extinction in some general way on 'the critics', since we had all been around long enough to know that this is what theatre people do indiscriminately, at all times and in all sorts of different circumstances. Yet when we laid the reviews out in front of us, there was an extraordinary pattern which brought us up short. It was as if a newspaper were able to be enthusiastic about us in directly inverse proportion to its influence. If you were, say, working for a small-town newspaper at least thirty miles from the centre of Manhattan, then you were apparently likely to consider *The Knife* 'a masterpiece', a word which was actually used – to make my point clearly – in *The Bergen County Record*. But the nearer your paper was to New York and the larger its circulation, the more likely you were to want to attack the show, with a ferocity which was only allowed to peak in the great mass circulation dailies. All our most impassioned admirers were in publications which had no direct commercial influence.

You begin in these circumstances to wonder whether it is coincidence that all your best reviews are in the wrong places. It is no doubt nice to be told by *Screw* magazine that you are much the most interesting and important musical of the season, but it is of very little use in building a regular theatre-going audience. Even as I read it my eye superimposed an unspeakable photograph of rather more graphic impact from the opposite page. But our suspicion that the official spokesmen of the culture were, so to speak, closing ranks was confirmed by the experience of Jack Kroll, the senior editor at *Newsweek* who was the only major critic to write a piece in praise of *The Knife*. He had only one problem. *Newsweek* would not print it. Week after week he tried to get it in. But because it went against the grain of received journalistic opinion, and because it was about a show which was not Officially a Success, *Newsweek* seemed reluctant to look different from everyone else. To publish would identify them not with the great cultural power-brokers at other major publications which they regard presumably as their equals, but with all the eccentrics and small-timers who were the show's declared supporters. We had a powerful sense of having broken a taboo.

We began in these afternoon sessions to try and work out what it was exactly that had occasioned such a violent response. We were, to begin with, unsure whether it was the form or the content. Two questions depress me more than any others in the theatre, yet they have punctuated almost every project with which I've been involved. The first, which is invariably well meaning and asked with a hopeful expression is 'Just tell me, what other play is this like?' The second, always put in a darker, more resentful tone is 'Yeah, but I mean . . . what do you want us to *think*?' The answers to these questions, which in the case of *The Knife* were 'Nothing else you've ever seen' and 'That's up to you', do not invariably satisfy. We were already different from most musicals in town. For a start we were not 'based' on anything. No book had been plundered. Nobody's life story was being told. No old movie had been painfully transposed. We were not hitching a ride on anyone else's vehicle, nor adapting from any other medium. We were, for better or worse, unfashionably ourselves, telling a fictional story in our own tone of voice. This, in itself, meant we were bucking every trend of the last ten years.

This meant we had always had the utmost difficulty in knowing how to advertise the show. There was no 'hook'. There was no 'concept'. There was no 'package'. The publicity department had prompted a series of impassioned arguments about whether we might be said to be a musical at all. Were we not rightly an opera? Every word of the libretto was sung. There were no spoken scenes. Yet 'opera' seemed the wrong word for a score so full of modern rhythm and melody, and which did, after all, break into things you could only call numbers. Audiences plainly were confused by the novelty of our form. But they were even more disturbed by our choice of content, or at least by its resolution.

The three of us had originally been drawn to an interest in our subject matter by the feeling that there are two things which mankind has uniquely been able to do in the twentieth century. He has created the means to extinguish the entire race to which he belongs, and he has developed techniques for a member of that race to experience life both as one thing and the other. Something which was once only possible in myth is now available to everyone, and, in England, what is more, on the National Health Service.

Getting to know a number of transsexuals we noticed they were inevitably rather absorbed in their own problems. They were on a crusade, and the subject of the crusade was their own gender. This made them often a little hazy in their appreciation of other people's needs and desires. They were not all that exercised by the question of whom they might hope to spend the rest of their lives with. Their most urgent priority was to get *themselves* right. Born with such an overwhelming sense of being trapped in the wrong body, they tended to see the operation as a release of their true selves. They often seemed unprepared for the fact that in freeing themselves they might cause untold unhappiness to their wives and children. They had to do something which was, for them, essential and right, something about which they effectively had no choice, but whose effect on others was catastrophic. As all our more perceptive audiences understood, the subject of our musical was not transsexuality but selfishness.

During the previews we began to have an inkling that perhaps some people were not as wholly at ease with the flavour of the show as we were. Our leading character, who is rarely off the stage, was played by Mandy Patinkin. In private life, Mandy is rather a highly charged man, whose conversation tends to erupt very suddenly, as if impelled, violently and with no particular warning, from deep inside him. There is a terrible sense of inner struggle, so that when words come, which may well be in the middle of your own sentence, they tend to be both extremely passionate and very loud. Mandy, bearing the brunt of this formidable show, was necessarily more alert to the audience's feelings than anyone, and he began to develop an obsessive conviction that the audience were profoundly discomfited by the ending of our story.

In *The Knife* the odd, lonely girl called Jenny (beautifully played by Mary-Elizabeth Mastrantonio) is the original inspiration for Peter's decision to become a woman, and it is her conviction and support which encourage him along his path. But, as the moment of the actual operation draws near, Peter becomes convinced that this is something he can only do by himself. The opening of the second act is a sustained duet, a long dramatic scene on the road to Casablanca, in which he violently rejects his hitherto closest ally. When the operation is done Peter–Liz tries to return home, but is, in turn, rejected by the family he–she has left behind. The feeling of the work becomes bitter and dark. Peter–Liz has done what she needed to set herself right in her own terms, but is left friendless and isolated. Towards the very end of the evening, there is finally a scene where the two women meet again beside a swimming pool. The scene comes late, just before the resolution, and it was on the outcome of this resolution that all Mandy's doubts began to centre. Jenny, embittered by her experience with Peter, is seen to have lost all hope of love and made an accommodation to middle-class life with an older and richer man. Liz is understood to be in desperate need of an ally. But Liz's sense of the pain she can still cause the still-pining Jenny brings her up short. She sacrifices their possible future friendship.

On the night of the thirteenth preview, I was dining at one o'clock in the morning in a perfectly regular Eighth Avenue bistro, when I was puzzled to be called to the phone by the *maître d'*. When I asked Mandy how he had managed to track me down so late, he told me he had first called my home, then every restaurant in an ever-widening radius from my home. The resolution of the story was, he had come to believe, a moral matter. Having presented an evening marbled with unhappiness and difficulty, it was absolutely essential that we did not let the audience go home without offering them the prospect of a reconciliation between our two major characters. Liz and Jenny must, in one way or other, go off together; not, he argued, in a sexual relationship (I was able to agree that a good lesbian love scene was the last thing we needed at this point) but in some gesture of affirmation which would imply that it was possible for these two very different people to spend their lives helping one another. Only if we made this point clear would we, he asserted, be 'satisfying' the audience in a way they needed; and not to 'satisfy' them would be to send them out into the dark night devoid of 'hope', which, he assured me, was an irresponsible and morally doubtful thing to do.

It is hard at this distance to do justice either to the unruliness or to the intensity of the argument that followed, my *steak frites* long cold and all the other customers gone home, while I, rather smugly, laid into the greatest lyric tenor of the American stage. In retrospect it is clear that changing the last moments of _The Knife_ would have done very little to charm the metropolitan critics into a keener appreciation of the show's virtues. There was always something unworldly about the project. As my girlfriend (she's American) said when the idea was first explained to her, 'You mean you're hoping to get to Broadway with a musical about a man who chops his cock off?' It was always her view that the show was horribly mistimed. Although the problems of transsexuals are entirely different from those of the gay community, she believed that _The Knife_ had no chance at a time when, because of AIDS, society was putting up its sexual shutters. But, even so, I found Mandy's line of argument uniquely illuminating, not just of _The Knife_, but also more generally of current orthodoxies in American culture.

Mandy was insisting that I had some sort of 'duty' as a writer and that was to help people by presenting stories which were in some way exemplary. It was as if I were a sports coach and my job was to send people back onto the track feeling good. Life was, after all, hard. If you went to the theatre and were asked to follow a character's journey, then you had some right to expect that at the end of that journey you would come out feeling that her struggle had been worthwhile. It was not fair to tell the audience that although the operation had solved Peter's problem with himself, it had done nothing to ease his relationships with others. It was, Mandy said, an article of faith in his own life that there was no obstacle which could not be overcome by two intelligent people, given goodwill and reason on both sides. The Jewish religion had tried to teach him that a certain amount of suffering was necessary and virtuous, but he had fought to escape that doctrine. People finally _did_ see their problems off and, as an actor, Mandy was only interested in appearing in works which made this plain. His argument was peppered throughout with personal reference.

He himself was, against all odds, in the manner of all New York, struggling to bring up his children in a city full of criminals and lunatics. He needed to pass something on to them: a conviction that however insuperable the difficulties of their lives might seem to be, there would always be some way through.

I must stress that at no stage did Mandy believe he was making a commercial point. He was not interested in anything as facile as a happy ending for its own sake. He was arguing that the theatre should be a place where people go for encouragement. He felt, as the actor who had to stand and sing at these sometimes surly and always anonymous people, that they were, in the last moments of the show, simply bewildered by a story which offered no immediate prospect of relief to its two heroines. They felt, in short, betrayed.

I was hardly in a position to disagree with his instincts about the way some of the audience were reacting. After the first performance a famous Broadway producer had remarked to Joe Papp, 'Perhaps you should only present the first act this season. I think that's all New York can take right now. Let them have the second act in 1988.' But as an English playwright who back home is generally accused of being over-moralistic, I was surprised to find myself in what seemed by contrast a rather reactionary position. It was left to me to point out that there are certain things in life which you can do very little about. Both Time and Chance play their part in human affairs, and neither is noted for its highly developed sense of justice. Two people may meet at exactly the wrong moment in their lives. Worse, they may find that although their temperaments are perfectly matched, their needs are not. Things may even reach the point where one of them decides that it is therefore wiser for them to part than to stay together. Both of them will be likely to experience an

inexplicable amount of suffering which may seem either pur-
poseless or malign. To remind an audience of this seems to
me not at all dispiriting, for it serves to illustrate what can
scarcely be said too often: that there is a great gulf between
what is true and what we would like to be true. To tell people
that certain problems in their lives are not only insuperable,
but may indeed be due to the operation of factors over which
they have no control, seems to me not a cruel but a kind thing
to do. And if they seem, as some of our audience did, unready
for this news, then I think we must conclude that other
writers have been stuffing their heads full of nonsense. A
suspicion may grow up that they live in a world where Piety is
more important than Truth.

I began after this late-night discussion on a telephone to
notice that there was indeed a prevalent policy of Official
Optimism. I also began to believe it to be corrupting, for at
least two reasons. It may limit what a writer is free to say – I
was effectively being asked not to write tragedy – but also it
may force him or her into gestures which are blatantly insincere. On a day off from the previews, I slunk away and sat too
close to the screen at *Platoon*. The film had considerable
integrity. It was made by a man who had plainly suffered a
great deal, and, more important, he had developed very clear
ideas on how he wanted to represent the terrifying degradation of war. But what was remarkable to any foreigner about
the film was its strange insistence that Vietnam was a pre-
dominantly American tragedy. Even after fifteen years it was
still impossible to offer any account of what had been done to
the Vietnamese themselves. In so far as they existed at all, it
was as yellow shapes to be blown off the screen. A great deal
was made of the damage the Americans did 'to ourselves'.
Nothing was said of the damage done rather more lastingly,
rather more woundingly to the large number of Asians whose

lives were forever changed or cut short by this foreign invasion. Imagine my astonishment when at the end of the film we were treated to a sanctimonious Piety in the form of a voice-over: 'In the hope that we shall never allow such a thing to happen again.' This hope was plainly a load of bull. There was absolutely no indication in the film that any force existed in the world which might make these soldiers stop and contemplate the consequences of their own actions. If such a force did exist, it certainly had not featured in the evening's entertainment. The sole purpose of this redundant homily was to transform the film into one which would be Officially Acceptable.

Living in New York as a visitor, you may begin to develop a creepy sense that the culture is being patrolled quite as rigidly as if you were stopping over in the Soviet Union. There are newspapers, appearing daily, which are out and about on ideological patrol, watching for bushfires, making sure daily obeisance is paid to 'survival' and success, while monthly restatements of the basic party principles are left to things called 'magazines', which carry stories of more private tribulations over which artists and actors have invariably triumphed. ('How I Beat Drink'. 'Why I'm Back with My Wife'.) Particular publications work to particular directives. The *New York Times* has plainly received instructions from Lubyanka that no story about the arts appears unless it is punctuated with dollar signs. 'First Novel Sold for $500,000' is a routine *Times* story. 'Actor Paid $3,000,000.' 'Cinema Tickets: Where your $6 goes.' A friend of mine had an article rejected on the grounds (I am quoting exactly) that 'You're trying to use the *New York Times* to put your point of view.' This was such an obvious violation of party orders that I wondered my friend had even tried.

The rhythm of party critics' work is annually climaxed by

the release of a new Woody Allen picture, which is judged according to just how many items of belief they are able to tick off in their Little Red Books. People have problems, *but they don't really.* Men are perplexed, foolish, neurotic and self-absorbed, *but women will always finally come across for them.* In *Hannah and Her Sisters*, a man falls in love with his wife's sister and then for no apparent reason goes back to his wife, *and suddenly it's all right.* Woody Allen's own character gives up his job because he is so exercised about the nature of existence. But unlike those people we know in the real world who are overcome by a sense of terror at their own mean-inglessness, Woody manages to maintain his ease and charm during his experience of unemployment. But anyway, he eventually decides, *Aw hell, what can you do?* and returns to the fold of New York society just in time for the infertile to become pregnant, and, for all I know, for the desert to turn a lush and fruitful shade of green.

I use the example of New York's best-known film-maker not because I think little of him. Far from it. He seems to me a talented man whose work has lost some of its power pre-cisely because he knows that he has been allotted the job of providing America with a fantasy of wish-fulfilment. He must tell them that out there, *everything is all right really.* When Allen tells them something else, as in *Stardust Memories* or *Broadway Danny Rose*, it is soon brought home to him that his work will be said to be less successful, precisely because it is more individual.

It is this paradox which seems to me at the heart of the decline of the American film industry, and the near-collapse of the legitimate theatre. A country which is supposedly devoted to the freedom of the individual seems set on insis-ting on a high level of conformity among its artists. As a writer on the *New Yorker* has observed, 'the rewards of not being different having never been higher'. This is strange, given that there is no longer any expectation that a Hollywood studio is likely to release a half-decent film. If one gets through, it is accepted that it will be more or less by accident. Most films arrive so chewed over by story committees and so clearly modelled on previous scenarios as to resemble nothing so much as cud which has been masticated and vomited by ten different cows. In the same way, there is no expectation that a serious play will more than occasionally either appear or survive on Broadway. The ritual of scraping together four titles for awards ceremonies becomes annually more embarrassing. There is no continuity of work for the absurdly gifted community of actors who would like to work on the New York stage. There is no remaining possibility of a classical career within a two hundred mile radius of Manhattan. There is no concept of what a theatrical ensemble might either aim for or achieve. Yet at no point do people who rightly lament this appalling state of affairs and who feel about it a grief far sharper than my own ever stop to consider whether the decline of their industries might be related to subject matter, and to what freedom is allowed to the artist.

I am not concerned to argue that a terrible injustice was done to *The Knife*. Who cares, apart from three of us who had, over five years, given a good deal of work to a show which lasted barely ten weeks, and who may perhaps be forgiven for feeling strongly? No, I am only concerned to record the lesson I learnt, and to ask two questions. The lesson is the same one I learnt when socialists demanded that my work be more polemical. There is a pressure in every society for art to be exemplary. It is far easier to be popular than to be true. To vested interests, the conclusion of a work will always be more important than the work itself.

And my questions?

Why does a country whose glory is supposed to be its diversity ask of its artists that they all become cheerleaders for the same philosophy? And is tragedy – that sense of watching something inexorable which no human being can intervene to prevent – now a forbidden form in the United States?

1987

14

A BIT OF LUCK
On *Paris by Night*

Sometimes as a writer you do get a bit of luck. I had spent the greater part of 1983 struggling with the script of my first feature film. Its themes were dark and its structure was formidably complicated. So I was very surprised to find myself back at my desk only one day after finishing it to set down a second, much simpler story which seemed to come like a free gift, an afterbirth to compensate for all the labour of *Wetherby*. It took me exactly six weeks to draft, and because it was about a Member of the European Parliament I called it *The Butter Mountain*.

For a short time *The Butter Mountain* appeared to be living a kind of charmed life, rather like the lottery ticket in René Clair's *Le Million*. I carelessly left the first script on a table in my living room, whence it was picked up, without my knowledge, by a visiting film producer. He then called me a week or two later to tell me that not only had he read it, but he had also shown it to a young man who happened at that time to be wearing the title of 'Hollywood's hottest director' (he has since made a film, and lost it). This man had meanwhile shown it to Twentieth Century–Fox who were keen to do what they called 'develop' it. This would mean re-tailoring the two central roles to fit neatly into the personalities and prejudices of two fabulously well-known actors. Fox realized, of course, that such a process would necessarily be bothersome and distressing to the man who had conceived of the original idea, so they were suggesting that in return for a sum of money, paid on the nail and delivered to my bank, I should have nothing further to do with the project. The sum they were offering was half a million dollars.

This is, I believe, the only mephistophelean moment I have enjoyed in my writing life. All playwrights take pleasure in frightening themselves with stories of financial temptation, but in fact in England (for example, at the BBC) the sums of money involved in 'selling out' are so pitiful as to represent no very grave test of character. It was Hilaire Belloc who defined the writer's two favourite dreams as 'the return of lost loves and great sums of unexpected money'. Yet I suffered not a moment's hesitation in rejecting their offer. I might as well have been asked to sell them a child. Perhaps if I had known just how hard it would be, and how long it would take to complete the film we renamed *Paris by Night*, I might have collected my money and fled to the hills.

I am told in Hollywood now the average period from when a film is first discussed to when the camera turns is three and a half years. *Paris by Night* took four. In peddling it round Wardour Street, I met at once with a familiar resistance. In answer to the inevitable question 'What's it based on?', I could only reply truthfully, 'Nothing. I made it up.' Films these days are so dominantly pre-digested, based on books which have been bestsellers, or little bits of newspaper which film-makers have cut out and pasted to their walls, that executives tend to come over queer when offered a script which is not based on 'facts' which they think they can hold on to. A startlingly low number of truly original screenplays now reach the screen. Once, realizing this, I bluffed a film financier by telling him that *Wetherby* was based on a story I had read in the *Yorkshire Post* about a stranger blowing his brains out in front of a schoolteacher. This blatant untruth instantly reassured him. For in the eyes of those who decide which films shall or shall not be made, there is no murkier or more unreliable place for a story to originate than inside a screenwriter's imagination.

There was a further commercial objection to *Paris by Night*, and that was of course that the leading role was written for a notably strong woman, and what's more one who was, in the cant phrase of the trade, 'unsympathetic'. Perhaps some day somebody will remember that some of the most successful films of the thirties and forties starred women doing unspeakable things, and moreover doing them with a relish to which the audience seemed ready to respond. Despairing after a year or two of seeking English finance, I was off begging in the United States, where I found an artistic orthodoxy quite as rigid as anything enforced by the commissars in Soviet Russia. On all so-called 'serious' projects (we may leave aside anything in the 'bash and slash' genre) it was an item of faith that the outcome of the story must be broadly 'optimistic' and that the leading characters must be broadly 'likeable'. It did not take me long to realize that *Paris by Night* was unlikely to be able to meet these criteria. Once, holed up in a nightmare hotel in Manhattan, I was asked by my producers to interview one of the two or three American actresses whose participation would have made the film an instant 'go'. 'I like the script,' she said, 'but I couldn't possibly play Clara Paige.' Reluctantly, I asked why not. 'Because she is so neglectful of her child.' I asked if this was something which, as an actress, she could not imagine playing. 'No way,' she said, showing me a lot of famous leg. 'You must understand, David, one day I'm hoping to have children myself.'

In fact it is my view that Clara Paige is not such a terrible person. Though the showbiz legislators could never admit it, she is not that different from you or me. When I went to Blackpool to see the new Tory woman, as it were, in captivity, I was struck by how much more generosity, breadth and soul I had given my principal character than was on immediate show in the simultaneously controlled and hysterical atmosphere of their Annual Party Conference. Although there has been a considerable body of plays and films about the economic results of Thatcherism, there has been almost nothing of consequence about the characteristics and personalities of those who have ruled over us during these last eight years.

It is one of the greatest mysteries of Thatcherism that it has generated so little fiction. In *Paradise Postponed* John Mortimer wove Leslie Titmuss into the national tapestry. But his friends and colleagues have long seemed seriously underrepresented. And no one yet seems to have written stories in which we are invited to work out just what it is that these strange people want.

Somewhere in the third year of searching, the film acquired a producer, Patrick Cassavetti, who had a formidable reputation for realizing difficult projects with very little money, and somewhere in the fourth it attracted the attention of Charlotte Rampling. I met her across a wide culture gap, made wider by a mutual ignorance of each other's work. Over lunch she praised *Wetherby* extravagantly. It was some months before I discovered she had never seen it. I was just as fulsome about *The Night Porter*, a film of which I have absolutely no memory. I also spoke well of *The Damned*, another film which I have somehow missed. After the meal, Patrick asked nervously whether we ought not perhaps to look at some of Charlotte's work before offering her the part. At the best of times reviewing an actor's earlier performances seems to me a highly doubtful and dangerous activity. If you don't know what it is that you, uniquely, want from an actor, then you should not be casting them. In Charlotte's case, a review seemed particularly pointless. She was being asked to contemplate returning to England after ten years' exile, to work with a writer and director of whom she knew very little, on a script which would show a side of herself which had scarcely been tapped in her previous career. For my part, I was guessing that, under the stereotypes of mad and bad that she was usually asked to play, lay a far more various and formidable actress. It was, in theory, a most spectacular gamble. And yet on a few days' acquaintance, I knew it was no gamble at all.

From the point Charlotte joined it, *Paris by Night* acquired purpose. It was no longer important it should be made. It was absolutely vital. For this reason, we went into pre-production without being properly financed, and twice faced weekends when we could not pay the wages. The first time, the American producer Ed Pressman stepped in to lend us the money to carry on. The second time, we ignored our problems and carried on with no money at all. Twice Patrick walked off, saying he could no longer hold the project together. I consoled him on the inevitability of his decision, but both times found him at his desk next morning. Nothing further was said. Just as the money did finally arrive, our first location was blown away in the terrible October storm. From the moment the camera turned, with the great British cinematographer Roger Pratt behind it, and a first-rate cast in front of it, I felt I was part of a team which had the power to make my writing as eloquent as possible.

In the fourth week, in the Halcyon Hotel in Notting Hill Gate, we found ourselves shooting the scene in which Clara lays out her philosophy of life to Wallace after they have made love. Clara is talking from her own experience, mixed up with a certain amount of confused political prejudice, yet a combination of things – the context in which she speaks, the tenderness with her lover, the play of light, Charlotte's exquisite conviction in the role – combined to produce in those of us watching a feeling of total disorientation. We simply did not know what our response to Clara was. We were watching a woman whose head was apparently full of careless and half-thought scraps, yet in the image of her and her own self-awareness was something so moving that you could not tell if beauty was confounding truth, or if the two, as I suspect they are in life, were so mixed up that nothing could unlock them. We were all robbed of our usual reactions. This is something I have so long wanted to do as a writer that a profound and lasting contentment came upon me, and it persisted through the remaining weeks of shooting. For as long as we worked, the process of art did what it has always promised: it comforted, it clarified, and set everything in order. A work and its reception are entirely different things and its making is a third. But this was one of the happiest times of my life.

1988

15

OH! GOODNESS
On *The Secret Rapture*

In the summer of 1987, just a few days after the Conservative Party won its third successive general election in Great Britain, I was, by chance, having dinner with a group of friends of my own age in a small village in Somerset. The man next to me was a well-respected novelist, whose books regularly competed for our most prestigious literary prizes. Over dinner he asked me what I did with my money. He said that as a playwright I must sometimes earn more than I spent. He wanted to know what I did with the excess. I replied that when I had extra money, I put it in the bank. He looked at me with open disbelief, and, laughing, said, 'Well, your bank manager must *love* you.' At this point he explained to everyone else at the table that he was sitting next to a man who kept his money in the bank. At once everyone joined in with a knowing kind of laughter, which left me confused. I asked the novelist what he did with his. He said that naturally, like everyone else he knew, he had a portfolio of stocks and shares. Each morning, before settling down to write, he spent an hour checking the movement of his shares and talking to his stockbroker. 'Surely,' he said, 'even you must have heard how much money people have been making on the stock exchange in the last six months?'

The point of this story is that, as the table fell silent, I realized that it was I, not he, who was way out of step with the mood of the times. Only a few years ago a novelist who began his day by scanning the *Financial Times* would have been a figure of universal fun. But now a playwright who was too stupid to know that a crazy boom was going on had become the contemporary figure of mockery.

It is perhaps the most remarkable of three Conservative governments' achievements to make any of us whose eyes wander from the main chance feel guilty and foolish for our lack of acumen.

No playwright of any value in my experience sets out to write a play *about* anything – or if he or she does the result is invariably disappointing. Yet something of the atmosphere of that dinner party did indeed begin to seep into me, and make me want to write. The flavour of the evening hung around me, like a scent. I found myself wanting to express the way English morals had changed so decisively during the eighties. I wanted to concentrate not on all the economic damage Thatcherism had done to the poor and the weak in Britain, but instead to show the subtle changes in the emotional lives of some of those who had apparently prospered under her government.

When *The Secret Rapture* was first presented in London, it was inevitable that it should be seen by commentators primarily as a political play. Foreigners are always shocked at just how bitter and divisive British politics are. And, in addition, I have often found myself exploring subject matter – the Chinese revolution, the role of aid in the Third World, the degradation of the British press – which involved me in the dramatization of ideas. The distinctive virtue of British theatre in the last twenty years is that it has not been frightened to address subjects of public interest. Yet when I finished the play, I believed it to be the most personal and private I had written.

My subject is goodness. Yes, I was interested to show what choices good people might have to make in order to survive or prosper among some of the other typical characters of the age. But I was also drawn to a more timeless theme. I wanted to show how goodness can bring out the worst in all of us. I had often noticed among good people that their effect on others was to make them feel obscurely rebuked. It had struck me how less virtuous people often feel that the good are criticizing them for their failings when, in fact, all they are truly listening to is the stirrings of their own troubled conscience. In Milton's *Paradise Lost*, God does not have to be powerful for Satan to become enraged. Satan is driven mad by God's very existence.

I am usually asked how much of *The Secret Rapture* is autobiographical, and I have to admit it was the death of my closest friend's father, and my experience of her grief, which first set up the opening image of the play in my mind. I started from there. But it is one of the great absolving mercies of art that anything which you take from real life will appear in fiction so wholly transformed as to be unrecognizable. In England in recent years there has been a depressing trend for justifying plays on the grounds that they 'really happened'. Our most heavily advertised films have been about people who 'really existed': Gandhi, Sidney Schanberg, John Profumo. *The Secret Rapture*, for good or ill, originated and developed inside my imagination. It is the most dangerous place to go for any story; but it has always been my source, and I am too old to change.

1990

16

FOUR ACTORS

Actors are right to be nervous. You can't stand on a stage without being judged. It's hard. The audience is judging not just what you do, but who you are. Of course they may sometimes get the two confused, but it may also emerge by the end of the evening, not just whether they like your performance, but whether they like you. The older you get, the more important the question of who you are becomes. John Gielgud and Ralph Richardson were loved because of the exceptional qualities they had as men. It was clear how they had lived. With Peggy Ashcroft it is the same. You can't avoid it. Acting is a judgement on character.

This does not mean that the good actor has necessarily to be a good person. But it does mean the shallow actor is caught out more and more as the years go by. The first person to make me think about this was Alfred Hitchcock, whom I met, as it happened, before I knew any professional actors. For a supposedly tricksy director, he had a very clear-cut view of the actor's relationship with the audience. He thought the audience loved Grace Kelly because she was indeed lovable. Although her beauty was cool, her ardour was not. Her own generosity shone through her work. He then talked about another leading lady whom he said he could not make the audience like, because, indeed, she had

no personal warmth. Likeability, like charm, was something
you could not fake. He said there was only one actor in the
world so brilliant as to be able to fake either. He also said I
would never be able to guess who it was. I was terribly upset,
because I didn't want to believe it, but I knew from Hitchcock's grin, which was not itself always kind, who he wanted
me to say. 'It's got to be Cary Grant,' I said. Hitchcock said,
'But of course.'

*

The common cliché is that film is just not an actor's
medium. The dull actor complains that on film he just
becomes a puppet, first in the director's, then in the editor's
hands. But he forgets that he has a far better chance than in
the theatre of offering an original performance, which
springs straight from his own imagination, and which has not
been mediated through a long process of discussion and
repetition. There is very little rehearsal on most films. The
actor appears on the set at eight in the morning and offers
something of his own to which the director, if he has any
sense, reacts. The director may build, but his starting point
is what the actor offers. In the theatre, an actor's original
impulse is just the starting point for a four-week-long attritional process of modification. Sometimes by the time
opening night arrives the actor's performance resembles a
trampled field. In the movies there's a much higher chance
of the actor's spontaneity retaining its vitality for all time.

On *Strapless* the casting director enjoyed a justified
moment of exhilaration, a few weeks before we started,
when she said, 'Blair Brown and Bruno Ganz! I just *know*
it's going to work.' She saw me looking nervous. 'Don't you
think so?' she said. I said I had no idea, and would have no
idea until they came out of their caravans on a Monday

morning. Nobody could know. If the contact was not there between them, it was beyond me to fake it. I was at their mercy. In the theatre, there are possibilities of disguise.

The actor's ultimate advantage on film is that he may communicate thoughts to the camera of which the director is unaware. However closely you're watching, you miss them. By definition, you cannot be placed between the actor and the lens. When you edit a film, then the subject and tone of a scene will take its colour from the scene which has immediately preceded it. A scene which has been shot for one purpose may, when re-edited, work even better in a place where it was never intended.

Often I find that an actor has got there ahead of me, so that when I slip the scene into its new place I find the actor's performance improves because the actor is having exactly the thought I now want from them. Because the material is alive in their mind, they are doing it without my previously having noticed.

Editing a film is, in part, the process of finding out what the actor was feeling at the time.

*

The experience of film and theatre directing is entirely different. The purpose of directing in the theatre is to impart knowledge so that the actors will one day be able to give their performances *in your absence*. For this reason, it is invariably exhausting. With luck the spirit of the work will be collaborative. But the movement of the work will always be away from you. Your job is to make sure that the actor knows enough, so that whatever situation arises on the stage he or she will deal with it in a way which is true to the spirit of the play. You therefore feel as if you're giving all the time. The point of the exercise is to give so much as to render yourself superfluous.

Of course, it goes without saying that on any worthwhile project you get a lot back, but at the end of the work you still feel drained.

When making a film, the movement is in the opposite direction. You are drawing in. You are collecting bits and pieces so as to hoard them away. The basic feeling is of people giving energy to you, not taking it from you. You need to be on the look-out all the time, taking anything you fancy from whatever department. You choose an actor who is not quite right for what you had in mind, but who offers a quality of their own which is more important and more lively than accurate casting would give you. You choose a location where the fall of the light offers you new meanings, or where the architecture will make the actors look good. Every morning you wake up nervous about how many bits you are going to get today. Once you have the bit, you have it for all time. You store it. The film is the sum of what you've stored.

*

Good films appear to happen under a glaze. It is as if a painter put varnish over the image at the last moment, and everything belongs. You should want to live in the world that the film creates. When I was a child, I didn't literally want to *be* Dirk Bogarde. But I did want to sweep through the wards as he did, and kiss the nurses he kissed. Unconsciously, when I write a film, the first thing I do is describe the light-source. I would never write a scene in a place where the light was going to be ugly. I also avoid places – airports, say – where there's unlikely to be an architectural feature which will give the shots style. Maybe you can make a stylish film in modern lecture halls, or in which actors get in and out of cars. But it's way beyond me. I can't shoot in places which don't seem to give something back.

One producer said I always spent a disproportionate amount of time worrying about what meals the characters were seen to eat. But when somebody comes up to me and says, 'Oh by the way, where is that restaurant in *Paris by Night*, because I'd rather like to go there ...?' then I regard it as the highest compliment. Unless the image has that sensuality, then your imagination is not seduced. The same quality must be there in film acting. The face must belong beneath the glaze.

*

Vanessa Redgrave

It's hard, when directing her, to know quite what Vanessa's doing. She has a very direct access to her own feelings and to the camera. She likes to talk a part through with you, but these discussions have very little bearing on what she will actually do. Most actors strain to find an emotion. They have to hunt around for it, and some actors, mostly American, make great play of the search for it. Vanessa seems to have some sort of plumb-line which takes her straight to the one she wants. It comes up pure. This is why she is the most admired actor among her peers. The feeling is always there.

She can also sustain a feeling longer than anyone else. In *Wetherby*, after a young man has shot himself in front of her, she has to come downstairs and face the police. After a while, she has to start talking about what happened. Any other actor would play the scene so that, at the appropriate point, you would see a change in their manner as they remembered the death. But Vanessa comes through the door with the death already written all over her face. It remains, in every apparently irrelevant line and gesture. Never at any moment in the scene are you allowed to forget.

Vanessa is hell to get to the starting line. She says she's

going to do your project, then when you ask around, you find she's got five others she's planning to do. All round London there are directors expecting to work with Vanessa in six weeks' time. It's as if it takes her a very long time to focus. Her bad eyesight physically heightens this impression, that she is someone wandering around in a fog. Rehearsals are therefore pointless. Or more accurately, they are pointless to you. But then when she does focus, the effect is more intense than with anyone else.

Judi Dench recalls that when they were at drama school together, Vanessa was a shambling and disorganized figure who gave little evidence of her future talent. The only class at which she then excelled was Restoration Monologue. It astonished everybody in the school that this chaotic young actor was the only one who could pick her way through this notoriously difficult discipline and make perfect sense. But it points to her other great strength: an exceptional lucidity of inflexion.

It takes you a while to understand that she won't say lines she doesn't like. Or perhaps she'll say them, but she won't give them any life. This accounts for the monotony of some of her screen performances. She is being asked to say things in which she does not believe, or of which she does not approve. If she does not think a line is true to her character, then she does not animate it. She just rides through, letting it become a dead patch, so that it has a curious, lifeless sing-song quality.

She wanted to do *Wetherby* because it gave her the chance to play a teacher. She has a real and heartfelt passion for youth. She feels the young suffer when adults do not give them their attention. She was therefore very concerned that Jean Travers come across as a good teacher, and she had trouble accepting that in parts of the script I had represented Jean as being absent-minded and vague, as though slightly dulled by the habits of loneliness. I was particularly proud of a line I had written when someone asks Jean if she has a television. She thinks for a moment, then says: 'Oh Lord, I do have one somewhere. Let me think.' Then she suddenly points to behind a pile of books. 'Oh yes, it's over there.' From the very first day these lines were a subject of contention between us. It amused me that Jean was so unworldly as not to be able to remember where her television set was. Vanessa found the line both unrealistic and out of character, or rather (since I created the character) out of what *she* wanted the character to be. For that reason she could never remember the line. When asked if she had a television, she would point at once to the pile of books and say, 'Yes, it's over there,' reducing the line to meaninglessness. Just to make the sequence doubly useless, she would go into her dead-computer voice.

This was not deliberate. One of the funniest aspects of this quirk was that it later began to obsess the composer of the film's score. Nick Bicât, by virtue of his job, has to listen to a film over and over as he works. He knew nothing of the film's making, yet his musician's ear alerted him to what had gone on during the filming. He would point gleefully to the screen and say, 'She didn't like that line, did she?' or 'Oh she didn't want to do that.' He was always right. He had developed a faultless gift for knowing when Vanessa was unconvinced of what I was asking her to do.

Actors who are not willing to 'have a go' are generally held to be bad sports, and worse. The director's first question is always 'Why don't you just try?' Vanessa never shows the slightest inclination to try, because she already understands something which a director does well to learn early on: that it would be no good if she did. It is not out of stubbornness that Vanessa will not do what she is asked. It is out of pure good sense. Unless it feels right, it will not work.

She has another passion. She wants things to be 'real'. Unfortunately, no two people agree on what 'real' is. A famous story is told of an actor who was instructed at the end of a run-through to 'be sexier'. He went to the producer and demanded the director be sacked, on the grounds that anyone who gave such a useless note did not know how to direct. And the producer agreed. I would suggest the same for any director who exhorts actors to 'make it more real'. It's a term with a thousand definitions. Vanessa's idea of real is that things look more convincing if they are tricked out with props. In a production of *The Aspern Papers* she asked Frith Banbury to release doves into the theatre, so that people would believe they were in Venice. You have to be quick. She infiltrates props into the action when your back is turned. 'Vanessa, what's that in your hair?' 'Oh, I thought it would be nice if she'd just picked up a flower.' The flower has gone in, like a flash, between the time the First Assistant calls 'Turn over' and I have called 'Action'. At one point, she had a flower in her hair, a pencil in one hand, a cup of coffee in another and she was also carrying a book. She fusses obsessively over these props. One day she was about to do the longest and most difficult speech in the film. 'Vanessa, what's that you're *eating*?' 'Oh, I thought it would be nice if she ate peanuts during the speech.' We went for a few takes with the rhythm of the speech destroyed by the irregular popping and crunching of the nuts. 'Vanessa, forget the fucking peanuts.' Far from protesting, Vanessa quietly put the peanuts down, looked entirely content and then delivered an absolutely flawless reading of the speech. Afterwards she thanked me for dealing with what she called 'the peanut problem'.

Her love of props comes, I think, from a desire to make herself ordinary. But many things about her – her height, her laugh, her myopia – are quite peculiar. And props will never disguise this. She is not, in that sense, a character actress. Her values are curiously nineteenth century. More than any-one I have met she believes in the great abstract nouns, with capital letters, like Youth and Enthusiasm and Wickedness and Art. These nouns are real to her, and inform all her acting. Her exceptional gift is for knowing what people feel, and having absolutely no sense of a dividing line between having a feeling and showing it.

*

Blair Brown

I do think women find acting easier than men. It costs them less. They seem less threatened by it. Most male actors, at some point, will look sheepish or angry and say how stupid it is to make a living pretending to be somebody else. It cannot be coincidence that so many American leading men have filthy reputations for being difficult to work with. In a sense, of course, they are just spoilt. The man expects the film to be about him. The woman expects to be given three or four scenes in which she either satisfies the hero, consoles him, or acts as his conscience. ('I do/do not think you're doing the right thing, darling.') One of the problems in casting my work is that the roles are reversed. The woman is usually at the centre of the story, and the man's role comments on the woman's. It's almost impossible to find leading men willing to accept this. All over the world there are actors unwilling to do for women what women have so often done for them. The whole apparatus of showbusiness, usually represented by agencies, is telling them not to. Women *expect* these roles. They spend their careers doing what I call 'pacing the cage': they are brilliant in the confined spaces of a few crucial scenes. Blair, like many, has spent a large part of her life pacing the cage. The interesting moment comes when she's let out.

On the screen the man expects to be in command. You have to put this down to insecurity. The actor wants to make the unmanly business of acting somehow look manly. When we were making *Strapless*, we came to an important scene in which Blair's character, who is called Lillian Hempel, will decide that she wants to marry her mysterious suitor, Raymond Forbes, who is played by Bruno Ganz. Lillian has had a row with her sister, and been to a ghastly medical party. She is sitting alone in her dressing gown, reading, when Raymond comes in. He asks how she is, and she tells him she's not very happy. As we were rehearsing, I suggested to Bruno that he put his head in her lap, to comfort her. The gesture seemed exactly right. Lillian stroked the back of his neck, and was freed by his not looking at her to let out all the things she has been nervous of saying.

After we had shot the scene, I noticed Blair was laughing and I asked her why. She said it was because of the way I had directed the scene. This was her first film in England, and she said no American actor would have agreed to do what I wanted.

I asked why not. 'Because putting your head in a woman's lap is a gesture of submission. They wouldn't allow themselves to be that vulnerable.' Astonished, I asked Bruno what he'd felt about this moment, of whose significance I had been totally unaware. 'Oh yes,' he said, 'I don't mind. It's fine by me. But I knew when I did it, I was just about the only film actor in the world who would.'

Blair's work is not all that well known in Britain. This is because she has the misfortune to belong to an exceptionally talented generation. Even if films were more geared to women's interests, no industry, however prolific, could produce enough good stories to accommodate the brilliant range of American screen actresses in their mid-thirties and early forties. Blair was first noticed in Ken Russell's film *Altered States*, where she played an anthropologist, married to William Hurt. She was then opposite Paul Simon in *One Trick Pony*. In *Continental Divide* she was a naturalist, protecting eagles in the Colorado mountains, and pursued by John Belushi. The British know her best for her impersonation of Jackie Kennedy in a mini-series where Martin Sheen played Kennedy. I imagine they cast her because she has the wide mouth and high cheekbones that make her look half-way between the President's wife and Rita Hayworth. Lately she has moved into a television series in a new genre, hideously named dramedy. *The Days and Nights of Molly Dodd* has her as a single woman on her own in New York, fresh out of a melancholy but powerful marriage with a saxophone player.

The extraordinary quality of her work is that she appears not to be acting at all. I am not talking here about the vulgar confusion in which the television audience assume that a character actually exists. It is the heartfelt conviction that the actor *is* the person they are playing, because you cannot see or sense the acting process taking place. I once mentioned Blair's name to a friend, who at once interrupted to say, 'I can't imagine someone called Blair actually existing, because to me she is just that doctor in the cancer hospital in *Strapless.*' I said yes, but she also appears in a television series in America, where she plays quite a different character. 'Oh I'm sure,' said the friend. 'But I haven't seen that.'

Blair does not achieve her effects by narrowing her range. She is not one of those actors who tailors every part to suit their own personality. I have always liked the story of Warren Beatty receiving the first draft of *Reds* and neatly dividing the script into two piles. The apprehensive screenwriter imagined Beatty was making some judgement on the quality of the writing. But not at all. Beatty pointed to one pile, 'Those are the scenes I can act.' Then to the other, 'And these are the ones I can't.' The story illustrates a profound understanding of stardom. The star must not get caught doing anything which makes him look foolish. He works inside his range. The scenes Beatty couldn't do were sent back to be rewritten.

By contrast, Blair relishes the untidy bits. She fights to keep in the odds and ends which don't quite make sense, because of course they heighten the sense that the person you are watching is 'real'. Her ease is all the more remarkable for the fact that it is not achieved through the lazy notion that film acting is about doing as little as possible. This dangerous doctrine is widely misunderstood. Once, on *Licking Hitler*, I was having trouble with an actor, new to film, who was standing in every shot looking as if he were a stiff propped up against the wall of a mortuary. When asked why, he said, 'Well, I'm told film acting's all about doing nothing.' I explained there was a difference between doing nothing and *thinking* nothing. The camera loves intelligence. It loves to detect what's going on behind the face.

Blair's gift for making everything look effortless and natural confuses American journalists who have written articles questioning whether what she does can properly be called acting at all. This may come as a surprise to English writers who have fallen into the lazy habit of assuming that American acting is more 'real' than what we see over here. On the contrary. When we watch the greatest and most influential of American actors, then never for a second are we unaware that we are watching Marlon Brando. He is usually putting on a display of technique which is quite as self-conscious as anything staged, say, by Olivier. It is dazzling, but *he* is always there. Whereas

Blair's gift is for seeming to absent herself. Another friend of mine was once embarrassed by watching her in a love-scene in a mini-series called *Space*. The fact that the rest of the series was produced and acted according to formula had heightened the sense that when this particular scene came, the viewer felt he was intruding. 'I mean, did she really need to give it that much?' All you had seen in fact was Blair's eyes as a man kissed her, but my friend had had to look away because Blair reminded you of how naked your eyes may be when you surrender. A moment later, the inevitable question. 'I mean, did she *really* fancy that leading man?'

There has never been a time in history when mankind spent so many hours watching himself. It is, if the word means anything at all, 'unnatural'. In another time, people might have expected to see twenty fictions in their lives. Now, by judicious switching of channels, you may see twenty in a day. The mass of material is overwhelming and it proceeds at a certain level of unreality. The actor's job has changed during the century from offering something fresh enough for the audience to recognize as life, to offering something *so* fresh as to blow away all the other enactments that come bubbling out of the television day after day. When this happens our first reaction may be one of alarm, and an obscure sense that the game is not quite being played by the rules.

There is an interesting scene in *Strapless* which evokes this very feeling. Lillian is so overwhelmed by her misfortunes in love and by the demands of her work in the hospital that she shuts herself up in a medical supply cupboard and refuses to come out. As she weeps helplessly, a black colleague comes to console her but is reduced to silence by his own powerlessness. One member of the audience told me that, watching this, she experienced something she had never known in the cinema: she herself became frightened to breathe for fear that any noise she made might intrude on Lillian's suffering. When the scene was over she realized that, out of respect, she had held her breath throughout.

What is this quality that bids us hold our breath? Why, a sense of privacy. A sense that what we are watching is not *intended* for our eyes. How is this achieved? Surely, not by instinct, but by years of refining your technique. Blair is one of the last American actors of an age to work their way through regional reps playing Shakespeare, Shaw and Oscar Wilde. She only went into films when she was thirty, with a small part in *The Paper Chase.* Nowadays, it is impossible to do ensemble work on the stage in New York, because so few actors have backgrounds in common. They meet at the first rehearsal. One has worked mainly in television, another has been part of a downtown mime troupe, a third has worked mainly in commercials, a fourth has had a brief, meteoric fling in films. The regional and national structure which allowed actors like Blair to experiment in public seems not to be producing graduates any more. In the theatre there is no continuity. There are just shows. Because of the cult of youth, actors are chucked into films, then chucked out again when their dimples fill out. The best ensemble work in New York is given by the hundred wonderful singers who go regularly from one musical to the next, season after season. They may work together all the time, and it shows.

Blair has also been allowed the rare luxury of getting to practise her trade. Every year, for the last three years, she has shot eight hours of film, all of which is, directly or indirectly, about the character she plays. With our stuttering industry, how many actors in England have enjoyed a similar privilege? One of Pauline Kael's cruellest jokes was about Alan Parker. 'He has technique to burn. And that's just what he should do. Burn it.' Blair has technique to hide. And that's just what she does. By hiding it, her own personality and the character's appear to become one. It's a glorious kind of acting. In fact, it's my favourite. But you have to have the personality in the first place.

*

Charlotte Rampling

Michael Gambon is the smartest and most experienced of actors, yet for reasons which escape me he hasn't made many feature films. Gerald Paige, in *Paris by Night*, turned out, bewilderingly, to be his first starring part. We would rehearse a scene, then maybe do a complicated two-shot (that's a shot with two actors in the same frame). Then we'd get ready for the close-ups. The convention here is that when it's not your turn, you stand close to the camera and help your fellow actor by repeating your performance off-screen. How much effort you make when you're not actually being filmed is usually thought to be a measure of an actor's generosity. Michael, characteristically, would give everything, every time. So I could see his astonishment when, one day, Charlotte Rampling asked him if he'd mind turning round, because she sometimes found close-ups easier when she played to the back of the other actor's neck.

Michael turned round, but I could see that he was thinking that this was vaguely unethical behaviour. After all, stage actors have it drummed into them that virtue resides exclusively in playing *with* your fellow actors. Acting is about contact. Only bad actors ignore the others. Charlotte did a couple of close-ups, and afterwards I saw Michael move towards her, intrigued. 'I don't know,' she was saying, 'I just find it liberating sometimes, not to be tied down to what the other actor is doing at that very moment. Besides, I can remember what you were doing, and I can now imagine what you are doing. So why not leave me free to work with imagination and memory?'

Fifteen minutes passed as we turned the cameras round. Michael was brooding by himself. When he was called to his place he said, 'Do you mind if I try this method?' Charlotte turned her back. We did some takes, and afterwards Michael grinned. 'It's against everything I've been taught and everything I believe. And it works.'

I asserted earlier that there is no way of knowing what is going to happen until the actors turn up, and that their feeling for each other is what makes a film begin to fire. And that is true. It's the *sine qua non*. But it is also crucial that everyone is at ease with the fact that a third person is present. In a love scene, any actor is necessarily two-timing, for the lover's performance is aimed, yes, at the beloved, but also, equally important, through the camera and out into the minds of the eventual audience. The tricky thing, as a film-maker, is to construct sequences which balance both needs.

I once asked Stephen Frears why the shooting-cycle of a certain director made his work seem so studied. Stephen pointed out how many close-ups this man was using. Because his background was in commercials, he didn't yet really trust himself with actors. So he avoided two-shots, because, Stephen said, in two-shots good acting cannot be faked. You either see it or you don't. Whereas if you shoot everything in singles, you can go back to the editing room and chop it all up any way you want, to try and intimate a contact which never occurred. Thinking about this made me realize why I find so much television so boring. The relentless close-ups make you feel obscurely cheated, because you are being hurried along by a false kind of energy, which just bangs up face after face, and misses out on what actually happens *between* people. Also, there is often no sense of the basic rules of editing. Shots should only be changed for a reason. Each cut should be there to give you a sense of forward movement. It must tell you, however subtly, that something has changed. If you simply cut back to a face which bears exactly the same expression as when you last left it, then you lose a sense of progress. You don't feel the story is developing at all.

The good film actor, then, has to be given the chance to work with the other actor, *and* to reach out beyond, into the dark. It is usually said of actors who have the second skill that 'the camera loves them'. Or else people say they have a 'film face'. Both terms are vaguely insulting. The best cheekbones in the world are of no value unless you know how to use them. Charlotte's beauty is treated as if it were a given. But no one knows better than she how to angle her head, or suggest a meaning by the smallest shift of her body. She understands just what the developed image will be, how the lens, the lights and the atmosphere will colour the content of the scene. This technique goes unremarked. Because she has lived in exile for ten years in France, the English have consistently under-valued her. She saw it as an irony of *Paris by Night* that playing a murderess nevertheless gave her a chance to show a more humane side of her character than all the smouldering sirens she is usually asked to play.

I admired both her technique and her unusual temperament. I noticed very early on that she always did whatever I asked. She explained to me that she had come to acting young, wrapped in the myth of the Kings Road and with nothing to lose. Because she had not done much else, she was not, at the beginning, overly serious about her career. She was therefore bewildered by how anxious and fretful many actors were. As she'd gone on, and her own ambitions to do good work had taken hold, she had begun to think that anxiety in itself usually had an inhibiting effect on your work. She watched actors who were limited by spending their lives in anger, either at others, or at themselves. Raging at their powerlessness made them even less powerful. So she made a conscious decision to work out what she wanted to do at home, and then take the day's film-making as it came. She was open both to what other actors and the director suggested. The result of this was that she made some bad films. But acting held no terror for her.

The vulgar response to this, of course, would be to say that here is the kind of actor directors most like. But this ignores two things. She always did what she wanted first. And she had an emotional card-index I couldn't fault. There wasn't a situation of the heart she didn't recognize. 'You know that feeling,' I'd say, 'when your son gets home late and . . .' 'Yes, yes,' she'd say at once. 'You know that feeling when you take the man home, and part of you still does want him, but the other part is thinking . . .' 'Yes, yes.' You can only be as relaxed as Charlotte if you have a wide experience. This means living a bit.

*

Anthony Hopkins

The problem of the theatre is repetition. Granville Barker wanted a National Theatre to remove commercial pressure, so that a production would only have to be presented fifty times. John Gielgud said fifty was as many times as you could do a play well. In the time he was at the National Theatre, Anthony Hopkins played Lambert le Roux in *Pravda* one hundred and sixty-eight times, and, breaking a record, he gave one hundred *King Lears*. Meanwhile he found time to play one hundred Antonys, with Judi Dench, in Peter Hall's production of *Antony and Cleopatra*. For two and a half years, in a twelve-hundred-seat auditorium, for all three productions there was never an empty seat.

If Charlotte's skill is for detaching herself slightly from her feelings in order to give herself the maximum room for manoeuvre, then we must say Tony is her diametric opposite. A novelist, in whose television adaptation Tony had appeared, said to me in a deprecating way, 'Tony seems to have no way of controlling his emotions.' There are two answers to this, only one of which I actually found to hand. One is: 'Yes, that's exactly what I most like about him.' The second: 'Yes, he does have a way. It's called acting.'

There are so many fanzines in the newsagents these days that it's hard to remember that a lot of people really don't like actors. They feel threatened by them. After all, an actor's job is to turn over the soil. Snobs don't like this. And they don't like energy either. On a good night Tony channels his emotions into displays of power and finesse which have no parallel in the English-speaking theatre. But he hates idling. He is bored when nothing happens in a scene. He's never content just to draw. He must colour as well. If he can't colour, he becomes impatient. The converse of his genius is that he has no way of hiding his distress if he feels a scene is not going to work. He is without guile. The most heartbreaking sight in the English-speaking theatre is Tony, standing there, bewildered, like a little boy, not knowing what to do while a scene goes down the pan. As always, he remains true to his feelings. His pain shows. In the novelist's terms, it is rank bad manners. The stage fills with a terrible sense of loss.

With Tony you expect a certain volatility. 'This is the best/worst production I have ever been in.' 'I've never loved/ hated anything so much.' In a dozen interviews, 'Dexter/

Hare is the worst/best director I've ever had.' After a show, 'That was the best/worst audience I've ever played.' The moment is everything. Nothing is more exhilarating than to see Tony in the wings, his arm round a fellow-actor, enjoying his companion's triumph just as much as his own, sweating from three hours' hard, physical work, make-up running down his face, his fists still clenched, and a big grin round his mouth. 'They didn't want the play,' he used to say at these moments, 'they didn't *know* they wanted it, but we rammed the bastard right down their throats.'

A brilliant mimic, his best anecdotes pivot on anger, righteous or ridiculous, as the case may be. When I hear Tony's voice in my head, it is usually saying the words 'I tell you, David, I was so bloody angry . . .' For every time he has been moved to protest at an injustice, he can name five when he has had to walk away and forbear.

I was always asking him to retell my favourite story which has him furious with a certain American leading lady for the way she was mistreating the technicians on a film they were making together. Deciding he would not tackle her without making sure he did a good job of it, he sat during the day's filming getting angrier and angrier as she was rude to one crew-member after another. Finally, he retired to his dressing room, where he spent the whole night, first writing, then memorizing a speech he would address to her first thing in the morning. When dawn came, he waited. When the camera was in place and the leading lady on her marks, he left the room and strode towards the set. As he tells it, his knees were shaking as he walked. When he got to his place, he looked her straight in the eye, and gave her the first line of his specially written speech. 'Let me tell you, *******, it's quite a good life if you don't *piss* on people . . .'

ME: (*Invariably*) How did she take that, Tony?
TONY: (*Very Welsh*) Well I think she was pretty surprised.

Looking back, the part of Lambert le Roux was always going to be one of Tony's zeniths as an actor. He accepted the part more or less sight unseen, on the basis of a sketchy First Act. He knew only that Howard Brenton and I were rewriting *Richard III*, reset in Fleet Street, and making fun of how the English say 'Oh, he's not as bad as I was expecting' when they meet their destroyer for the first time. By a stroke of luck, which suited Tony's gift, there was not a single moment in it in which he was limited to doing one thing at a time. At every point he could pour in some primary feeling, spite, say, or a lurid kind of charm, which made each moment gleam with promise. His hair slicked down, he looked reptilian. Was this the *shiniest* performance an actor ever gave? Night after night, he would try to pump in more power, push the sense of the character further and further. When Peter Brook deserted the English theatre to go to Paris and work out what theatrical experience was, I thought he was losing his mind. But watching Tony every night, I sensed a practical man straining to answer the same question Brook asks. 'How can I make every night as good as the last?'

For this is the question no one can make sense of. The theatre should be special. The only point of it, now that so many alternatives are on offer, is that something extraordinary should happen. How can you make something extraordinary happen spontaneously, yet on cue, every single night of the year?

When *King Lear* was about to open, I gave Tony some half-arsed director's note, which sounds deplorable out of context but which – if you will believe me – was indeed the appropriate thing to say at the time. It had been an erratic rehearsal period, sometimes white-hot with excitement, some-times debilitating and unclear. The power we had found in the rehearsal room vanished as we moved onto the stage. There were some listless previews, as if the company were seen behind glass. I felt, rightly, that Tony was over-awed by playing the eleven wildly diverse scenes Shakespeare assigns to the King. He had forgotten our original conviction that from the moment he appears, Lear is alive to the implications of his own actions. The one thing I understood about the play is that Lear knowingly brings his tragedy upon himself. He sets off on a great experiment, announcing his deliberate intention to 'crawl unburdened towards death'. For once Lear was played not as a doddery old man (Tony never once shook or trembled in the role) but as someone deliberately pushing human experience to the ultimate. The result was that when Tony walked out on the first night, a wonderful sensitivity and melancholy hung about him, as if in giving away his kingdom he had a presenti-ment of the tragedy ahead. From that moment on the King became unbearably sad.

When I went round afterwards to congratulate him on his unexpected success, I found him depressed. He said he had done what I had asked. He had brought his own suffering onto the stage. And it had worked. A heavy role had in that instant seemed light. 'Now,' he said, 'I have that performance. The one I shall give when the juice is there. But it can't be every night. It's humanly impossible. And until you start speaking you have no way of knowing which kind of night it's going to be.' He looked at me. 'And I still don't have the technical performance, the one that will *just get me through.*'

We ask so much of actors. Every night they must do it – just for us. We grow angry and impatient when they fail us. Yet in the theatre we ask that every night they conjure up a mystery over which – however good they are – they do not ultimately have any control. Once an actor has prepared and has the role in his grasp, then every night the bird comes down and settles on his shoulder. Or it does not. Unless he develops a certain insouciance about the bird's behaviour, the actor easily becomes a troubled man. Yet often in his troubles, there is a courage which moves me very much. On the last night, after one hundred, I asked Tony what part he would most like to play next. 'King Lear,' he said.

*

Once, years ago, when we were doing *Plenty*, Kate Nelligan had a speech where she had to describe one night of love with a man who was then killed in a concentration camp. As she said the words 'men dying naked in Dachau', she invariably cried. Julie Covington, playing another part, watched her for most of the run, fascinated, and asked her how she managed to cry in the same place every night. She asked if there was a trick to it. How could the actor learn to do it? What did Kate think of to make herself cry? Did she think about the death of someone close to her? Did she think about the saddest thing she knew? 'No,' said Kate, 'I'll tell you what I do. I think about men dying naked in Dachau. I just think about them. And then I cry.'

*

I have spent twenty years watching actors, talking to actors, spending evenings in actors' company, and trying to work out what actors do. Tonight, as I write, I can imagine Tony playing his Steinway, Blair reading her favourite novel, Vanessa handing out pamphlets on the picket line, Charlotte dining in the French *beau monde*. After all the time I have spent looking at them, I could not save my own life by plausibly acting one single scene. The sadness of the lover comes when he or she realizes that, however much they love, they cannot *be* the other person. Nor can they ever really know what the other person feels. The Great Pretenders depend for a living on the fact that everyone is different. But by drawing the person they are playing in towards their heart, they also bring good news. The best ones tell us everyone's alike.

1990

APPENDIX
Works by David Hare

Plays

SLAG: produced in 1970 at the Hampstead Theatre Club, with Rosemary McHale, Marty Cruickshank and Diane Fletcher; directed by Roger Hendricks Simon. Subsequently revived at the Royal Court Theatre in 1971, with Lynn Redgrave, Barbara Ferris and Anna Massey, directed by Max Stafford-Clark. Produced by Joe Papp in New York at the New York Shakespeare Festival in 1971, with Roberta Maxwell; directed by Roger Hendricks Simon.

THE GREAT EXHIBITION: produced in 1972 at the Hampstead Theatre Club, with David Warner, Penelope Wilton and Carolyn Seymour; directed by Richard Eyre.

BRASSNECK: written with Howard Brenton; produced in 1973 by Richard Eyre at the Nottingham Playhouse, with Paul Dawkins, Jeremy Wilkin, Jonathan Pryce and Jane Wymark; directed by David Hare. Subsequently produced as a Play for Today on BBC Television in 1975, with Paul Dawkins, Jeremy Kemp, Andrew Ray and Susan Penhaligon; directed by Mike Newell.

KNUCKLE: produced in 1974 by Michael Codron at the Comedy Theatre, with Edward Fox, Kate Nelligan and

Douglas Wilmer; directed by Michael Blakemore. Subsequently presented as a Theatre Night on BBC Television in 1989, with Tim Roth, Emma Thompson and Bernard Hepton; directed by Moira Armstrong.

FANSHEN: based on the book by William Hinton; produced in 1975 by the Joint Stock Theatre Group on tour and at the ICA; directed by William Gaskill and Max Stafford-Clark. Subsequently revived in 1975 on tour and at the Hampstead Theatre. Subsequently revived in 1977 on tour and at Oval House. Presented in a television production on BBC2 in 1975. Subsequently revived by the National Theatre at the Cottesloe Theatre, 1988; directed by Les Waters.

TEETH 'N' SMILES: music by Nick Bicât, lyrics by Tony Bicât; produced in 1975 at the Royal Court Theatre, with Helen Mirren, Jack Shepherd, Dave King, Cherie Lunghi and Tony Sher; directed by David Hare. Subsequently revived at Wyndhams Theatre in 1976 with Helen Mirren, Martin Shaw and Dave King.

PLENTY: produced in 1978 at the National Theatre, with Kate Nelligan, Stephen Moore and Julie Covington; directed by David Hare. First produced in the US at the Arena Stage Washington in 1980, with Blair Brown, John Glover and Joan Mackintosh; directed by David Chambers. Subsequently produced by Joe Papp at the New York Shakespeare Festival with Kate Nelligan, Ed Herrman and Ellen Parker in 1982; directed by David Hare. Subsequently transferred in this production to the Plymouth Theatre in 1983. Subsequently filmed in 1985 with Meryl Streep, Charles Dance, John Gielgud and Tracy Ullman; screenplay by David Hare; directed by Fred Schepisi.

A MAP OF THE WORLD: produced in 1982 at the Adelaide

Festival by the Sydney Theatre Company, with Roshan Seth, Penny Downie and Robert Grubb; directed by David Hare. Subsequently transferred in this production to the Opera House, Sydney. First produced in the UK at the National Theatre, with Roshan Seth, Diana Quick and Bill Nighy; directed by David Hare. Subsequently produced by Joe Papp at the New York Shakespeare Festival in 1985, with Roshan Seth, Liz McGovern and Zelko Ivanek; directed by David Hare.

PRAVDA: written with Howard Brenton; produced in 1985 at the National Theatre with Anthony Hopkins, Bill Nighy and Tim McInnerny; directed by David Hare. This production revived in 1986 with Anthony Hopkins, Richard Hope and Peter Chelsom. Then revived again, in 1986, with Anthony Hopkins, Bill Nighy and Christopher Baines. First produced in the US in 1989 at the Guthrie Theatre in Minneapolis; directed by Bob Falls.

THE BAY AT NICE and WRECKED EGGS: a double-bill produced in 1986 at the National Theatre with Irene Worth, Zoë Wanamaker, Colin Stinton, Kate Buffery and Philip Locke; directed by David Hare.

THE SECRET RAPTURE: produced in 1988 at the National Theatre with Penelope Wilton, Jill Baker and Clare Higgins; directed by Howard Davies. Subsequently revived in 1989 with Susan Tracey, Diana Hardcastle and Anna Calder-Marshall. Produced by Joe Papp in New York at the New York Shakespeare Festival in 1989 with Blair Brown, Frances Conroy and Mary Beth Hurt; directed by David Hare. This production subsequently transferred to the Barrymore Theatre in 1989.

RACING DEMON: produced in 1990 at the National Theatre

with Oliver Ford Davies, Michael Bryant, Adam Kotz and Stella Gonet; directed by Richard Eyre.

Films for TV

LICKING HITLER: presented on BBC TV as a Play for Today in 1978, with Kate Nelligan, Bill Patterson, Hugh Fraser, Brenda Fricker and Clive Revill; produced by David Rose; directed by David Hare.

DREAMS OF LEAVING: presented on BBC TV as a Play for Today in 1980, with Kate Nelligan, Bill Nighy, Mel Smith and Helen Lindsay; produced by David Rose; directed by David Hare.

SAIGON: YEAR OF THE CAT: presented on Thames TV in 1983, with Judi Dench, Frederic Forrest, E. G. Marshall, Wallace Shawn, Roger Rees, Josef Sommer and Pitchit Bulkill; screenplay by David Hare; produced by Michael Dunlop and Verity Lambert; directed by Stephen Frears.

HEADING HOME: presented on BBC TV in 1991, with Joely Richardson, Gary Oldman, Stephen Dillane, Stella Gonet and Michael Bryant; produced by Rick McCallum; directed by David Hare.

Films

WETHERBY: made by Greenpoint Films in 1985, with Vanessa Redgrave, Judi Dench, Ian Holm, Tim McInnerny, Susannah Hamilton and Joely Richardson; produced by Simon Relph; directed by David Hare.

PARIS BY NIGHT: made by Greenpoint Films, with Pressman Productions, in 1988, with Charlotte Rampling, Michael

Gambon, Ian Glen, Jane Asher, Robert Hardy and Robert Flemyng; produced by Patrick Cassavetti; directed by David Hare.

STRAPLESS: made by Strapless Films in 1989 for Granada Film International, with Blair Brown, Bruno Ganz, Bridget Fonda, Alan Howard, Rohan McCullough and Suzanne Burden; produced by Rick McCallum; directed by David Hare.

Opera

THE KNIFE: music by Nick Bicât, lyrics by Tim Rose Price, book by David Hare; produced by Joe Papp in New York at the New York Shakespeare Festival in 1987 with Mandy Patinkin, Mary-Elizabeth Mastrantonio and Cass Morgan; directed by David Hare.